MOTIVATE YOURSELF TO IMPRESS
HOW TO MAKE 'EM LOVE YA' AND PICK YA'!

MOTIVATE YOURSELF TO IMPRESS
HOW TO MAKE 'EM LOVE YA' AND PICK YA'!

College Students' Guide to Getting Hired

Leave an imprint on every mind you encounter.
Leave your mark on every project you oversee!
Leave your current and future boss wanting more!

KATRIKA STERLING-HAMILTON

To order additional copies of this book, contact:
Xlibris
1-888-795-4274
www.Xlibris.com
Orders@Xlibris.com
731676

CONTENTS

Acknowledgements

I dedicate this book to my mother Ruthlyn Rowe Harvey, who died from breast cancer at age 42. She was truly the wind beneath my wings. Although her death was untimely, I made her a promise to leave my mark on the world. I honor her memory and the many sacrifices she made; her death ultimately propelled my professional education and career. To my father Dudley Romer, I honor you. I also dedicate this book to my husband and companion Andrew Hamilton, children Ramah and Elijah, and to the many students who have inspired me to take my teaching beyond the classroom.

My faith also inspires me. I thank the Lord for giving me the strength to accomplish this project. I hope this book will inspire students, professors, employees and employers. We live in a world where you have to be willing to go beyond the norm if you are going to leave a mark. I hope I have accomplished this.

Thank you to my siblings, Camille Williams, Jose Spurgeon, and Brittany and Tracie Harvey for your prayers and encouragement. Special thanks to Professor Susan Lichtman and Celia Grell for proofing and editing my work. It was hard work creating a better flow. Finally, thank you Apostle Steve Lyston for encouraging me to write my first book. Words are not enough to extend my profound gratitude for all your encouragement, support, and words of wisdom.

Any views or opinions presented in this book are solely those of the author. The informational questions, answers, resume's and cover letters are hypothetical responses. They only serve as a guide. I recommend that readers conduct additional research as it pertains to your desired career field. The author is not responsible for any inaccuracy.

Foreword

Professor Katrika Sterling-Hamilton, despite her youth, is a venerable educator, enlightening both her students and colleagues on how to more effectively present their ideas and themselves in academia. Her experience and expertise in the business world and in the college classroom inform this helpful, informative and entertaining handbook on how to get the job of one's dreams.

This book is more than just a "bag of tricks" or a collection of dry, outdated tips that would have perhaps worked in the 20th century. This particular book enables its readers to get a realistic view of the ever-changing job market of the 21st century, making clear the point that one must adapt and see the interview from the standpoint of those who hire the prospective employer.

Although this handbook instructs, it entertains as well. Professor Sterling-Hamilton makes good use of pop culture to illustrate the character traits, skills sets and training that prospective employees must have to obtain their professional goals. She invites her readers to engage their imagination, to think creatively and to focus on their goals. She helps her readers to see that there are specific, feasible things that they can say and do to impress their potential employers and therefore enhance their chances of getting the job of their dreams.

This handy book provides a sort of road map that will help people who are entering the job market (and those who are considering finding a new career path) to navigate their way through the job seeking process—from writing the resume to performing well in the interview. The book is a sort of mini-course, the type of course that is both instructive and enjoyable.

Ronald E. Walker, Associate Professor Senior
Department of English & Communications
Miami Dade College, North Campus

Introduction

"You've got to commit yourself to an act or vision that pulls you further than you want to go and forces you to use your hidden strengths." - John Johnson

I was born in Freeport, Bahamas and migrated here in the 1980s. I attended Miami Gardens Elementary School and transferred to Carol City Senior High School (a tough school, by-the-way). I wasn't raised with a silver spoon in my mouth. My father was a hardworking man, and he was and very strict. My father was the type of man who was going to make sure that we did what we were supposed to do. To tell you the truth, his belt intimated me. I thank God for him and because of his sternness, I was able to keep my eyes on my cheese. Spencer (1998) in his book, *Who Moved My Cheese*, says we each have an idea of what 'cheese' is and we pursue it because we believe that it makes us happy. If we get it we often become attached to it. If we lose it, or if it's taken away, it can be traumatic. Since you are holding this book, I can tell you are on a quest for your cheese. With my help, *YOU* will find your cheese. Cheese represents finding your voice, your dream job, the right mate and/or success in the corporate and private sectors. Spencer's book discusses four characters that fought their way through a maze in order to locate their cheese. This book will help you navigate through the employment arena so you can land your dream job. Can you smell your cheese? How does it look? What does you career opportunity look like? Is it bite sized, small, large, or beyond what your mind can conceive? Do you have a road map to guide you to your job success? Do you have a mentor? This book can serve as a roadmap and a mentor to your success.

So I left the Bahamas and came to Miami when I was about eight years old. I didn't know my life would be a quest for 'my cheese.' I never had things easy. I am a product of the harsh field life in the Bahamas; I learned to pick potatoes, to plant corn, and to catch chickens. I also learned the pain of being rejected and even the horror of having my innocence taken at a very young age. You name it,

I have experienced it for the most part, but it didn't make me weak. I learned and survived it all. I like what poet/author Langston Hughes says in one of his greatest pieces *Mother to Son*:

"Well, son, I'll tell you:
Life for me ain't been no crystal stair.
It's had tacks in it,
And splinters
And boards tore up,
And places with no carpet on the floor
Bare.

I think many people can relate to these words. Life is a challenge and it gets difficult, but it also can be good. I saw my mother telling the same things Langston depicts in this poem. Have you ever had a parent who beat now and asked questions later? HELLO! My mother-Ruthlyn Rowe Harvey (affectionately known as Bev) was going to make sure I attended college. She didn't want me to get attached to materialistic things, and getting pregnant was not going to happen in the Harvey household. My mother raised five children on her own without a man being present. She loved the Lord Jesus Christ. He kept her sane even when life seemed to go from one storm cloud to another. She was the greatest role model, doctor, nurse; you name it, my mother was it. She didn't have a formal education, but she had wisdom. I am sure many of you can relate to this based on how your parents raised you. I learned through her pain, problems, heartbreak and yes, the cancer that eroded her body, that life is whatever you make of it. You have to determine in your mind that you are created for something greater and that your eyes have not seen it yet; neither has it entered into your soul the things the Lord has in store for YOU! She would say, "Baby, this too will pass." That really kept me alive after she died.

My mother was a woman who wore an armor that not even cancer could penetrate. Ruthlyn was the greatest no-nonsense woman who made sure I kept my head on straight and into the books. In her native Jamaica she didn't have it easy; she had to quit school to help out with the household chores and bills. However, although she didn't have a formal education, we never went hungry. My mother would say, "I don't have the money to send anyone to college; you have to get there the old fashioned way." So I kept my head in the books and made sure to earn grades that would make colleges want to look at me. I graduated from Miami Carol City Senior High with a 4.0 GPA. I wanted to show my mother that what she invested in me was going to be realized in the next generation. Colleges and universities from all over started writing to me from Cornell University and Stanford University, to the University of Miami and Florida State University. I didn't know what to do. I could pick, choose, and refuse. I chose Miami Dade College simply because of its location and mission. The key words that stood out in its mission statement were "accessible, affordable, and high quality education" while keeping students at the center of the decision-making process. I knew I was headed in the right direction.

Today, I am a professor, sought-after motivational speaker, pastor, communication consultant, and now, author. As a result of my professional experiences, networking opportunities, failures and successes, I write this book to edify, share, and empower students, teachers, practitioners, and organizations with successful ideas, tips, strategies, and practices for employment purposes. There are four guiding principles to this book, outlined as follows:

1. **Develop An Impressive Outlook**
    An impressive outlook allows students to see their future from a different cultural perspective. These days, a good job is hard to find. But that won't be a decent excuse for a slim résumé when you're sitting across from an employment recruiter next year. Like it or not, college students are expected to be capable of pulling good grades in tough classes while gaining professional experience on the side.

2. **Develop An Impressive Appetite**
    The statement, "*you are what you eat,*" really is true. Partying, drinking, and having lots of fun can slowly create an obstacle between you and your dream - you become handicapped to what you must face. Before you know it, five years have gone by and you are still at the starting line. Then you lose interest and something else takes up all your time. It is difficult to get back into the game if you can't remember the players. Therefore, research programs, networking events and continuing education in your specific field should be fundamental. Do you read educational books? Do you attend seminars? Do you provide voluntary service to certain organizations that can open the door to a potentially permanent relationship?

3. **Develop An Impressive Vision**
    Rather than having a macro perspective, the student with an impressive vision looks within and begins to uncover his or her unique gifts and qualities. The student quickly understands that his or her ability will separate them from the pack or they'll get "left behind". Their vision is so immense that they always have their heads stuck in the clouds. That student senses there must be more and like a mouse in a maze, begins the search. It is that drive and desire that helps create a connecting bridge to their purpose and allows them to propel into places they can only dream of.

4. **Develop An Impressive Mindset**

    The United Negro College Fund's motto, established in 1944 states, "A mind is a terrible thing to waste." Don't be afraid to dream big dreams. Take advantage of what your college campus and even this country have to offer and then pursue it with intensified zeal. Seek knowledge, don't be afraid to ask for help if you need it and listen; you don't need to know it all, but find someone who can help to direct your path. Remember, your thoughts are connected to what you say verbally. Develop an attitude of excellence that distinguishes you from the ordinary to the extraordinary.

I have taught for over fifteen years at Miami Dade College and two years part-time at Nova Southeastern University. I have been exposed to countless situations where students became frustrated because of a presentational flop or when they had a job interview and were not able to articulate clearly. So if that's you, welcome to the club! I was one of those floppers. College students are graduating at an alarming rate but not necessarily getting hired into their particular field. The National Association of Colleges and Employers survey (2009) reports college students are leaving campuses with fewer jobs in hand than their 2008 counterparts. The group's 2009 student survey found that just 19.7 percent of 2009 graduates who applied for a job actually had one. Can you believe that? Finally, with future careers leading into the STEM (science, technology, engineering and mathematics) fields, students will need to be able to compete for top jobs. But don't worry; I am convinced that *Motivate Yourself to Impress* will help you connect the dots before, during and after the interview, along with helping you understand some of the current changes happening in Corporate America.

The **purpose** of this book is to help college students acquire lasting career opportunities. It is also geared towards educational facilities and the role they play in preparing 21st century workers. Book knowledge is one thing, but application and strategy are critical to breaking through the doors of corporate America. Presenting what you have learned in the classroom through service learning or internship programs will double your chances of getting hired by a company. In this book, you will learn **five fundamentals** to help prepare you for your dream job:

1. **YOUR** thinking can make you or break you
2. **YOU** have to transition from the classroom to the corporate boardroom
3. **YOU** are the product
4. **YOU** will learn the tips, strategies and techniques for corporate success
5. **YOU** will be empowered!

Your end result will be summed up in three words: **"You are hired!"** You will discover the latent potential inside of you. Your voice needs to be heard. Your ideas need to be taken into consideration. Your presence and what you have to offer **will not** be denied.

Chapter 1

HAVE A W.I.T. MENTALITY

"Whatever I tell my mind, it will perform" - K. Sterling-Hamilton

What does W.I.T. mean? Do you have a *W*hatever *I*t *T*akes (W.I.T.) mentality? Are you a willing, intuitive, tenacious individual that is able to compete in corporate America? Alan J. Kelly, president of ExxonMobil's Fuels and Lubricants Division, suggests that in order for college students to compete they have to do the following:

- **Know Yourself** - Kelly stresses the importance of self-awareness when making decisions and figuring out next steps. Many opportunities may look attractive, but some (National Association and Colleges and Employers, 2009) are ill-advised because they may not fit your personal philosophy or within the context of your larger life plan.

- **Work to Build Capacities** - Kelly urges college students to develop a variety of marketable skills and talents that will enable them to compete in this increasingly competitive global environment. He drives home the point that "being good is not good enough anymore."
- **Develop Influencing Skills** - Alan Kelly explains to students that collaboration and relationship-building are two crucial skills in today's corporate landscape. He adds that almost no one works in isolation and a person's ability to effectively work in a team is directly correlated to his/her success.
- **Create, Connect and Convince** - If you are going anywhere in life you must be creative in your approach and must think cutting-edge. You should also be able to network, be a team player and convince your potential boss within the first 90 seconds of your interview why you are the ideal job candidate.

A fifth criterion I am adding is **Service Learning**. According to the Institute for Civic Engagement at Miami Dade College, service learning combines classroom pedagogical learning and real world experience. It helps to establish a strong foundation in practical applications to theory-based courses; it meets academic, social and civic learning goals, and brings awareness to some social ills organizations face daily. This type of learning is also essential because it teaches students about the role they play in developing strong community relationships. Service learning provides students a "better understanding and real-world application of the course material." It allows students to engage with current issues and social problems, and to work with community organizations to become part of the solution. Now, let's envision how the criteria mentioned above can help you develop your skills, interests, and qualifications in order to compete in corporate America.

"For being different, it's easy. But to be unique, it's a complicated thing." – Unknown

OUR THOUGHTS

Everything we see in this world began with a thought. Everything we perceive in the physical world had its origin in the invisible inner world of our thoughts and beliefs. The scripture states that God spoke, "Let there be..." and it was. According to Webster's Dictionary, a thought is "an idea or a mental picture, imagined and contemplated." Imagine for a minute the beauty, eloquence and splendor of the Eiffel Tower. Before this magnificent structure was created it was just a thought. It was chief engineer Maurice Koechlin (an employee of Mr. Eiffel)

2

who came up with the structural concept and form. He was light years ahead of his time and well versed in structural concepts and techniques. He had a progressive mindset. When he approached French engineer Gustave Eiffel with this idea and concept, it was sure to be a success. The project was name after Gustave Eiffel because he had the money to back it. What began as a simple thought developed into a 1,063 foot structure; it went through 5,300 blueprints, took 50 engineers to work on it and approximately two years to build.

So again I ask, how far is your thinking? Your thinking should be like a farseeing telescope. Simply put, our thoughts are powerful. Before an idea becomes a reality it often goes through many changes. Our thought system governs everything we do and will receive in life. So let's turn the light switch on to powerful thoughts.

POWERFUL THOUGHTS EQUALS POWERFUL IDEAS:

As college students, I know you have a lot on your minds and on your plates. Juggling four to five classes, working part or full-time, and maintaining healthy relationships can be a daunting task. You may be married with children or bear the burden of taking care of siblings, grandparents, etc. I understand you have a load to carry and a lot to balance at the same time. Consider the following as you begin to grow in your profession. Your **M-I-N-D** has to be ready and stable to move to the next level of your career.

M-Maximize Your Creative Potential Daily. Creative insights sometimes come in a blast or bit-by-bit. What can you do or bring to the corporate environment? What is needed in the organization? Do you see and know it, but are just too afraid to step out and offer the suggestion? Learn to minimize your doubts, kill your fears, believe in yourself and step out of the box. Connect with "creativity accelerators." According to Gottschalk (2013), creative accelerators are those individuals who explore and develop ideas to help create a successful marketing image. These individuals may not seem to have much in common with you but can help with your ladder to success. If connecting with "creative accelerators" isn't possible, begin to create a "core" group of people who have the mindset to make the leap.

A great example of "creative accelerators" is the late Apple mogul, Steve Jobs, who started his company in 1976 with his friend Steve Wozniak. Another partner in the company, co-founder Ronald Wayne, feared financial ruin so he relinquished his 10 percent stake in the partnership for only $800.00. Apple then launched a series of products like Apple III, which was at first a success but then failed to meet customers' expectations. It was too big, the motherboard would overheat, and it crashed constantly. This didn't stop Jobs. The company moved into the "creative accelerator" direction and in 1984, introduced the Apple Macintosh.

This computer was like no other because it was self-contained, including the display, and had an easy set-up. The company did go through some major rifts that led to Jobs resigning. However, in 1998, there was a "rebirth" of Jobs' vision and he continued to nurture "creative accelerators" with the iMac computer and the Internet. The iMac cleared away legacy technology, including the ubiquitous floppy disk drive, and emphasized networking and getting online easily (Jade, 2011). Since then, the Macintosh production (MacBook Pros, MacBook Airs, iPads, iPods, iPhones, Apple Watches, plus much more) has excelled at innovation and dominated the technology industry.

I-Information, Information, Information is Paramount to Success in Your Career. Knowledge, experience and wisdom yield powerful results. Do you like to read? What are the changes in your career field over the last five years? Believe it or not, knowledge is power. The more you know, the more competitive you are and the higher are your chances of acquiring a career that matches your ability.

Are you a self-starter? Are you a quick learner? Are you able to adapt? What does your career entail? Learning about changes in your career field is vital. You don't want to spend time earning a degree just to find out it is useless. Are you versatile? Do you make connections? According to Sharee (2013), connecting with the right person and market can improve your life financially, professionally, and socially. It may be an hour-long interview, a five-minute introduction at a meeting, or a casual encounter with a stranger at a party. To get started, you should always have a minute long "past, present and future" speech about yourself defining what you've done, what you do, and what you're interested in doing. Think of it as a condensed version of your Facebook profile page, leaving out your fondness of Keyshia Cole and your favorite *Friends* re-runs.

N-Negative Thoughts and Negative Beliefs are cancerous to your vision. They will always affect your success and opportunities. You attract what you think and say. Have you ever said, "Today is going to be a great day, I can just feel it." Before you know it the day manifested exactly as you said it would. Conversely, have you ever said, "I just feel terrible, I know something awful is going to happen?" Guess what? What you spoke came to be. Even if there are reasons to feel this way, speak life. Proverbs 18:21 tells us "Life and death are in the power of the tongue." Additionally, our minds are like sponges. A sponge has multiple purposes: it absorbs, wipes, rubs, and cleans. What you absorb is what comes out of you.

Hanging around negative people will lead you off a cliff or hanging on to one. In the article, "Zig Ziglar's Lessons from the Top," by Erin Casey (2008), P.C. Merrell, president of the company for which Ziglar sold cookware in the beginning of his professional career was said to have pulled Ziglar aside following a sales meeting and said these words to him: "I have never seen such a waste of time and effort." With a puzzled look on his face, Ziglar asked, "What do you mean?" Merrell replied, "I believe you can be a great one in this business if you would just believe in yourself, work on learning more, doing better and helping other people." As the story goes, Merrell's words of advice were a turning point in Ziglar's career. Encapsulating those words, coupled with the training he'd received, within a year Ziglar went from barely scraping by to becoming No. 2 in a company of more than 7,000 salespeople. He later reached the No. 1 position in another company of more than 3,000.

Are you just scraping by? It's so easy to become critical and negative, especially if you have been on five job interviews and haven't been hired yet. You become complacent and decide you can't be bothered with looking for employment any more. People sometimes resort to blaming others, blaming the system, or blaming their skin color or race. These may be factors, but it's the limitations we put on ourselves that is the root cause of stagnancy, unproductivity, mediocrity, and failure. How I begin is one thing; what I become is another.

D-Develop and Hone Your Talents and Your Abilities. You are unique, distinct, and rare; you cannot be replicated, duplicated, or imitated. Find out what you are good at and work it. The late great businessman, author, entrepreneur and motivational speaker, Zig Ziglar, said, "Believe in yourself, dedicate yourself to continual learning and to helping others. I repeat: You can have everything in life you want if you will just help enough other people get what they want." What a powerful statement! You can have everything if you just help others get what they want. Putting others' needs on the same level as your own creates a win-win situation.

Developing "self" takes time, work, energy, and sacrifice. Ziglar said, "You need to be a constant student because things change and you have to change and grow. I emphasize the word *grow*. If you keep learning new things, the new information—so many times—strengthens what you already know. As a professor, I believe class should always be in session. Developing yourself is both physical and spiritual. Balance is crucial to the developmental process. Once the process is set in motion, your will to succeed becomes inevitable.

WHAT ARE YOU LOOKING FOR - A JOB OR A CAREER?

What's the difference between a job and a career? The terms *job* and *career* are often used interchangeably. However, there are important differences between the two terms. Let me describe it this way, if you are dating a person for a while and things are good, you may suggest taking the relationship a step further. The person looks at you and says, "Why ruin a good thing with marriage? Having a monogamous relationship will only spoil things." Listen, this is a temporary relationship. There is no true commitment. The moment something else comes along that looks better this person will jump ship.

This can happen with a job, too. Have you ever worked for a company and someone else was hired but paid more for the same job? You are tempted to do what?! Yes that's right, interview at the other company. I know I would! When there is no solid commitment in a relationship, anything goes. When you don't have a degree, your job can easily be given to someone else who is more qualified. Jobs are a means to an end. They are oftentimes temporary. You need it to pay your bills, books, tuition, classes, and even your rent. Even though some jobs lead to careers, they are often task-oriented positions to help meet the goals of an organization or business. That's like you working hard in a relationship, investing quality time just to find out they are marrying someone else.

A Job Opens the Door but a Career Keeps it Open!

A career is long-term. Can you see yourself working in the same field day after day, week after week, month after month, and year after year and not getting burned out? Can you see yourself growing, transforming, and empowering others around you to perfect their craft? A career is about longevity. Let's go back to my relationship example. In a relationship you both are committed, your goals are the same, you are loyal, and you are sold on each other. Singer extraordinaire Beyoncé Knowles sings, "If he loves you he will...what?" That's right, "Put a ring on it." Your career seals your future. Renowned psychologist Abraham Maslow suggested in his hierarchy of needs that self-actualization is the need which is at the peak of the pyramid. Maslow describes self-actualization as a person's need to be and do that which a person was "born to do." "A musician must make music, an artist must paint, and a poet must write." At the peak of this hierarchy is self-actualization.

Maslow's hierarchy suggests that when the other needs (physiological, security, social, and esteem needs) in the pyramid have been met, an individual can then focus his or her attention on this pinnacle need. Self-actualization is described as "...the desire for self-fulfillment, namely, to the tendency for a person to become actualized in his potential. When you graduate from a college or a university, nothing can remove the degree you earned; nothing can take away your credentials as a nurse, an engineer, a business administrator, a doctor, a lawyer, a teacher, etc. That degree is yours until death do you part! A career is something that you build during your lifetime. The people you socialize with, the networking functions you attend, or maybe even the service learning experiences you participate in form the foundation that serves as a launching pad to your career. Maybe as you read this book you are unsure of the path to take. Begin researching, begin seeking. Get suggestions from your college campus career advisors on which path to take.

Sit down with that favorite instructor and allow him or her to help you construct a strategic plan that will get your career vehicle in motion. One of the worst things any student can do is take classes in a field in which they are not interested. I am not talking about the prerequisite classes everyone has to take those; what I am referring to is spending your time and money in a career field that you dread and the end result is finding yourself in a dead end job. Famous inventor George Washington Carver spoke at Selma University in Selma, Alabama on May 27, 1942 and in concluding, he made this statement:

> You are the handicap you must face. You are the
> one who must choose your place,
> You must say where you want to go.
> How much you will study the truth to know,
> God has equipped you for life, But He
> Lets you decide what you want to be. Look them over, the wise and great,
> They take their food from a common plate
> And similar knives and forks they use,
> With similar laces they tie their shoes,
> The world considers them brave and smart.
> But you've all they had when they made their start.

Carver was a humble man who asked God to reveal to him the secrets of the universe. Carver jokingly exclaimed that God said that was beyond his range and expertise. So God revealed to the young scientist the secrets of a peanut. Do you know what he was able to do with that little peanut? Dr. Carver researched and developed more than 300 uses for peanuts including chili sauce, shampoo, shaving cream, and glue. He had many struggles due to race, segregation, and working with limited resources. But this didn't prevent him from expanding his ideas, developing his skills and abilities, and becoming a great distributor of his products. He was an educator, a scientist, and a humanitarian living during a time of racism and segregation. He was exposed to the horrors of lynching and lived in a segregated society, but his mind was not enslaved. He was able to push pass societal labels and earn his master's degree in agriculture. He was a pioneer and his ideas about sustainable agriculture based on renewable resources were lightyears ahead of his time.

You are your greatest motivator and greatest obstacle. You have the ability to turn the place upside "right" where you decide to expand your horizons. Yes, I said upside "right" instead of upside "down." How many times do you hear people and companies selling certain products or goods and you become drawn to one more than the other? Do you shop at Wal-Mart or at Publix? Why, you may ask? What is the difference? The difference may be the price of the goods, how they are promoted or even how they are packaged. When you walk through those doors to interview for a position, why should they buy into your ideas rather than another candidate's? Basically, you must somehow influence the company, the board, the department, the community, the nation, and even the world. A career is something that should excite you and propel you to expand your knowledge, best practices, best skills and best talents, and fit your lifestyle. Career development is not something that just happens in a career class in high school or when you begin looking for your first big job. Career planning is the ability to look ahead and think about where you are going and what steps you will need to get there. Building a career unfolds over one's lifetime with bits and pieces of it happening every day.

BITS AND PIECES COMING TOGETHER

Piece 1- What would you do even if you were not paid?

_____
_____
_____
_____

Piece 2- Why are your studying a particular major? What outcome do you expect in the next 2-3 years?

_____
_____
_____
_____

Piece 3-With whom do you network? It's not just *who* you know, it's *what* you do about who you know. According to U.S. Department of Labor Statistics (2004), 63.4 percent jobs come from networking. List your networking contacts and follow-up.

_____
_____
_____
_____

Piece 4- Will your career field grow within the next five years? Or ten years? How? What will be some of the driving forces?

_____

_____

_____

_____

I know you have heard these questions a thousand times but they bear repeating:

What are you good at?
In one statement finish this thought, I am good at _____.
What drives you? I am driven by _____.
What is your greatest fear? My greatest fear is _____.
What is your greatest weakness? My great weakness is _____.
What motivates you? I am passionate about _____.

DIFFERENT STROKES TO THE WORLD

"We are all born originals; why is it so many of us die copies?" –
Edward Young

You have heard the saying different strokes for different folks. Different things motivate different people. If you ask Oprah Winfrey where her motivation came from she might say her humble beginnings. She suffered humiliation and ridicule. She was raped and abused at the hands of those who were supposed to protect her. She went through mental, emotional, and physical trauma. Yet she had grit. If you ask someone who has been out of work for six months and has a family, what is their motivation, they will say it's their family. If you ask a recent graduate about their motivation, they might say that it's "finding my space in the corporate arena and leaving a legacy." Your motivation is crucial to your career success. But inspiration is crucial to discovering what you are passionate about.

I remember when I graduated from Carol City Senior High I felt life could only get better. I had a lot of friends who had gotten pregnant and made poor choices about their future. I had a few friends who made the right decision and they are gainfully employed today. Some made the mistake of putting their college dreams on hold.

I didn't have a choice. My mother said, "You are going to college." I didn't have time to relax. I graduated in June 1992 and started attending college full-time that same month. By the way, I had an advantage; I was enrolled in Miami Dade College's dual enrollment program for law enforcement since the 11th grade and there was no stopping now.

However, my love for communication came when I took my first speech course. Professor Gwen Fuller was teaching SPC 1026 (now SPC 1017) and she was exceptional. Her voice, body language, and how she interacted with the students were so captivating, I simply wanted to "be her." But I realized there could only be one Professor Fuller. Each of us is unique, distinct, and cannot be replicated, duplicated, or imitated. There is only one *YOU and* YOU do *YOU* so well! So, I set out on a quest to find my identity, to find my flare and knack for public speaking. I would still major in the field of communication, regardless of pay. I loved it that much! I saw the effect I had on people and how their lives changed because of a peak performance seminar I facilitated, a speech course taught, or a corporate workshop training I led. I loved the feeling of empowering individuals to accomplish their next great move. I sometimes get emails from students saying, "Professor, I was hired;" or "Professor, it worked, I got the scholarship."

FREE YOUR MIND AND THE REST WILL FOLLOW!

On September 24th 1993, the song "Free Your Mind" from the group En Vogue's critically acclaimed album *Funky Divas* debuted. The whole point of the song was to rid yourself of prejudice and stereotyping; to stop letting others think for you; to not be shallow or read into things that are not there. A mind that's not free to create, explore, write, think, or dream becomes frustrated, tunneled, and eventually dies.

A free mind is a healthy mind. Have you ever had so much on your mind that you could not function? College students struggle with so much information overload and there is only so much one's mind can take. My mother was struggling when I started Miami Dade College. I was stressed because I had too much coming at me all at once. I had to take my mother to chemotherapy, watch her cry every night in pain, watch her beautiful hair fall out, watch her 205 lbs. body be reduced to 100 lbs.; watch her beautiful caramel complexion turn "dark" black. I was scared, angry, torn but was able to hold it together mentally because of my mother's strength, and most importantly, my faith in my savior, Jesus Christ. If you can go through something like I have and still maintain your composure and not lose sight of your goals, you have the sharp focus of an eagle. If we can do these things, bearing up under the most intense pressure, we *will* transcend ourselves, and we will also--in that moment--find a way of conquering self-doubt, fear, and control over the human spirit.

The mind is made up of thoughts, memories, imagination, and consciousness. The *thought* is a mental process which allows individuals to model the world around them. It also helps to develop their goals, plans, and visions. The *memory* is a person's ability to store, retain, and subsequently recall information. Information is first placed in your working memory. This is the part of the consciousness that interprets and assigns meaning to stimuli to which we pay attention. Information once interpreted in the working memory is sent to either the short-term or long-term memory. Your short-term memory is similar to post-it notes because you remember it briefly, but then you forget. The long-term memory is like your super computer (Pearson, 2011). The long-term memory "serves as your permanent storage place for information including but not limited to past experience, language, values, knowledge, memories of sights, sounds, smells and even fantasies." Then, there is *imagination,* which is the ability to form a mental image of something that is not perceived through the senses. It is the ability of the mind to build mental scenes, objects or events that do not exist, are not present or have happened in the past. The word *"conscious"* is derived from Latin *conscius* meaning "having joint or common knowledge with another, privy to, cognizant." "Anything that we are aware of at a given moment forms part of our consciousness, making conscious experience at once the most familiar and most mysterious aspect of our lives"(Schneider and Velmans, 2007).

As you can see, the mind is a very complex. College students experience things like no other groups on the planet. Your mindset in the classroom is the determining factor of how you grasp the information you have been taught and your application of it in the world. Learning how to navigate successfully through college to keep it free from "mental clutter" is not easy. Say you are driving along a road and you feel a bump, but you don't pay any attention to it. You continue to drive, then you go over a pothole, feel a strong thud, and before you know it you have a flat tire. This is among the most common and important traps to be aware of. The smallest stumble or setback can often be enough to bring a complete end to any plans for change. Likewise, our mind operates that very same way. We must train the mind into not only knowing but also believing that any bump in the road is simply a learning experience, a tool you can use to readjust your thoughts and proceed with greater insight and intelligence.

Having a whatever-it-takes mentality should be the cornerstone to success of every college student in the workplace. Webster's Dictionary defines "mentality" as, "the sum of a person's intellectual capabilities or endowment." What are you good at? What comes natural to you in your college classes? These are some clear indications of where you need to start exploring. If you're good at math, consider a major in accounting or financial planning. If you enjoy science and experimentation, consider a career in the occupational health care field or in research. If you are a good advocate, debater or revel in resolving disputes, a career in law could satisfy your appetite. If you are nurturing, compassionate, and have a passion for health care and health education, the medical field is where you belong. If you relish working with figures, making money, have great problem-solving skills and an ability to lead small or large groups, then consider a career in business. Maybe you like taking things apart, are always reading about technological advancements or simply have a compassion for computers, then engineering or computer science are where you're headed.

On the other hand, if you are as undecided as I was when I first entered Miami Dade College, then I do understand if you are basically clueless of what your next action step will be. I knew I was outspoken and loved communicating, but needed guidance. It was not until my first speech class at Miami Dade College (which by the way was very intimidating), that my instructor suggested that speech communication would be my cheese!

"The cheese is important in the maze; it pushes you to explore, investigate and examine possibilities." – Katrika Sterling-Hamilton

Listen! You are cut from a different cloth. Your thoughts, traditions, and world perspective are different. The way you carry yourself reflects the kind of connections you will make. W.I.T. individuals refuse to be denied. They refuse to have a speech impediment, an accent, a physical impairment, or even poor communication skills as a road block to their success. Kimbro (1998) states, "The road to success is cluttered with obstacles" and you have to know how to drive your vehicle (passion in your field) to get to your desired destination. You have to be able to tap into your purpose…work hard, be positive, don't look back, and take a bit at a time.

Wally "Famous" Amos was the type of person that never looked back. If you like cookies, then you have to taste the formula for success that he pioneered. In every job, Wally "Famous" Amos always started at the bottom and worked his way to the top, but that was not his passion. He wanted more, so he found a new hobby - baking chocolate chip cookies. Baking relaxed him and made him reminisce about his Aunt Della's cookies. Wally wanted more. In 1975, long before there were "food personalities" and chefs like Emeril Lagasse, Paul Newman, and Nigella Lawsohn, Amos came up with the idea that he could sell his cookies and become an entertainment personality. Of course he was told every possible reason why he should not pursue his passion. Opening a store would prove unprofitable. Calling the doubters "haters," "aggravators," and "debaters," Amos followed his dream and did what he was called to do. His face, tied to the Famous Amos brand, was a huge success. What would have happened if he had he listened to the doubters and dream killers? Today, we enjoy eating his cookies. Even though he had minor setbacks, his business blossomed and the rest is history. His passion became his career.

EASIER SAID THAN DONE!

"That's easy for you to say!" you may be saying; "You don't know how I was raised." "You don't know that I've been incarcerated for five years and still have no idea what my future holds!" "I just lost a friend in another shooting." "Do you know I have three children on welfare and am fighting the system; I can hardly make it to school because I have no bus fare." You may even be saying, "Professor, I struggled with grammar and English as a second language?" My answer to all these thoughts is, you are able to overcome anything if you are driven!

I can relate to every scenario mentioned. *Remember I grew up in Carol City* and boy oh boy, don't I know what it is to depend on government cheese. I know what it feels like to struggle with writing, reading, and grammar. I know what it feels like to lose friends to gun violence. Picture this: your mother drops out of elementary school because she can't read. She then gets pregnant and sends you to live with your father. Your father can't handle the extra mouth to feed so he sends you to live with your grandparents. While there, you are molested several times without a clue why this was happening to you. You are treated like the black sheep, and had daily field work. Your bathroom is outside, literally outside where everyone can see. So you have to hide and bathe. There is no running water or place to shower. That's the kind of lifestyle I lived. These humble beginnings have helped me establish a strong foundation. All things work together; the good, the bad, and the ugly, as stated in the Word of God in Romans 8:28. I hold no one hostage in my mind. I have forgiven every act, deed, word and abuse. I am free.

When your mind is free from what people think about you, feel about you, and say about you, you can handle rejection even from a job interview. You are able to use that experience, learn from it, let it go and apply again.

IMPRESSIVE PROFILE: RUTH SIMMONS

Ruth Simmons grew up during the time of segregation in Grapeland, Texas. She was the youngest of 12 children. When required, her father and the whole family worked as share-croppers in the cotton fields. It was a time of brutal segregation in the south. Her earliest memories are of being told to step aside when a white person approached, and never to answer them back.

"I very quickly became socialized into believing I was worthless," she says. "Grapeland was the kind of small, east Texan town where blacks got murdered if they stepped out of line." Things looked up after the family moved to Houston when she was seven. "The neighborhood was shabby, there were bars on every window, and crime and alcoholism were part of the daily routine," she says. "Yet I was blissfully happy. People bothered to insist I go to school, and I loved it. There was a calm and an order that was missing elsewhere in my life. But, above all, there were books. My parents were deeply suspicious about my reading, but for me it opened a window into a different reality, where it was possible for someone like me to be accepted."

As a child Mrs. Simmons spent hours in the kitchen watching her mother shell peas and shuck corn, soaking up her lessons about living right. That was a special kind of education, but Ruth had bigger dreams; she wanted to go to college. Her mother could make no promises. She told her if she earned a scholarship then she could go to college. Deep down inside she knew her mother still doubted her ability to obtain a scholarship. Unfortunately her mother died, but now it was time for Ruth to venture off to college. With very little money and borrowed clothes, she charted unknown waters and racism to go to Wellesley College in Massachusetts and the cultural gap between the other students and herself was huge.

Today, Mrs. Simmons is the first Black President of an Ivy League institution, Brown University. As an academic leader, Simmons believes in *the power of education to transform lives*. She champions the university as a haven of reasoned debate with the responsibility of challenging students intellectually and preparing them to become informed, conscientious citizens. She has spent her career advocating for a leadership role for higher education in the arena of national and global affairs.

A W.I.T ASSESSMENT

You have to take a step even if it's a difficult one to take. Accept no restrictions. The road Simmons chose was extremely difficult. Racial segregation, lack of resources, and low self-esteem were the prevailing themes in her academic life. However, she refused to accept reality for what it was. I really don't know where you are in your academic study or your financial status as it relates to your classes, but one thing I do know – you climb the ladder step-by-step.

Face it and Make it Happen. You will be faced with every road block, ditch and pot hole that will prevent you from achieving your next level. Cry, then get over it. There are some things we have no control over, such as race, height, family background, death, betrayal, etc. Life sometimes brings us lemons, but we should be smart enough to make lemonade. Simmons couldn't help the fact that she was born during a time of racial injustice and that her family was barely able to make ends meet, but she understood fully what it was like to be humiliated. She turned the unexpected into an opportunity for growth.

How we handle the inevitable changes in life is key to living a life without fear. The right attitude can mean the difference between allowing unexpected life changes to keep us from achieving our goals, or dealing with the changes and growing because of them. Motivational speaker Chris Clarke-Epstein puts it this way: "The most constructive thing you can do with no control factors during change is (1) Recognize they exist, (2) See them for what they're worth, and (3) Let them go."

Leverage Your Strengths: Ruth Simmons took a position that has been dominated by men. Simmons took over as Brown's 18th president and became the first black president of an Ivy League university and one of a handful of female presidents leading elite research institutions. She viewed limitations as possibilities. She took a position that so many would not be able to handle, due to the pressure, the long hours, and more. I believe she embodied this quote, from the great actress Cicely Tyson: "Challenges make you discover things about yourself that you never really knew. They're what make the instrument stretch-what make you go beyond the norm." Find out what you are good at and work it!

Chapter Reflection

My Cheese

Name it _____

Where are you in your journey? _____

How long will you have to be in the maze? _____

Which company holds your cheese? _____

I learned that my MIND has the ability to...

_____

_____

After reading this chapter...

I am _____

I am _____

I am _____

What is my W.I.T.? How will I assess it?

_____

_____

_____

_____

Chapter 2

BRIDGING THE GAP

"The first step to closing that gap is to believe, as I do, that high expectations are for all students. I believe intelligence is equally distributed throughout the world, but opportunity is not. And the same is true within our own country." -- President William J. Clinton

GAPS BETWEEN INSTITUTIONS - STUDENTS AND CORPORATE AMERICA

In their article, "Across the Great Divide Perspective of CEO's and College Presidents on America's Higher Education and Skills Gap," Bridgeland, Milano and Rosenblum (2011) say businesses are desperate to hire; however, less than "53 percent of employers find it difficult to find qualified workers." The economy is moving at a snail's pace, says Bridgeland. Employers are seeking talented, qualified workers while employees are seeking organizations that will hire with benefits. There seems to be an underlying current showing that our students are not as prepared to handle the challenges of the future, so let us see what the research says about today's students.

One finding is that the skills gap is expected to intensify with the gradual departure of the "baby boomers" from the workforce. While many older workers are postponing retirement because of the recession that began in 2007, it is still estimated that approximately 77.2 million will leave the workforce over the next two decades, resulting in an overall loss of expertise and management skills (ASTD, 2009). Unfortunately, experts say the way college students are being trained is a harsher reality; many business owners say that unless the skills gap is reduced significantly they will be forced to continue to look for qualified workers outside the U.S. In today's economy, more than two-thirds of the positions are require high level skills, (Gordon, 2009). By 2020, three-quarters of the job market will require high-skills and only 26 percent will be for lower-skilled individuals. The implication is plain: If America wants to remain competitive, we will have to expand our supply of highly skilled workers (Gordon, 2009). To remain competitive as a nation, the gap between the knowledge and skills needed by employers and the number of available workers who meet those qualifications must be addressed. The American Society of Training and Development (ASTD) defines this "skills gap" as "a significant gap between an organization's current capabilities and the skills it needs to achieve its goals." It is the point at which an organization can no longer grow or remain competitive because it cannot fill critical jobs with employees who have the right knowledge, skills, and abilities. In a recent ASTD poll of 1,179 organizations, 79 percent reported a skills gap within their organizations.

Another issue is the gap between employers and educational institutions. This seems to pose the greatest concern. The ASTD article reports that because of this gap students are not finishing their degrees. A recent inquiry by the McKinsey Global Institute (2011) expressed skepticism that the U.S. could achieve full employment before 2020. More importantly, the authors are emphatic that "better matching of workers to jobs" must accompany sustained demand growth and more global competitiveness by U.S. companies. Among MGI's key findings:

> Under current trends, the U.S. will not have enough workers with the right education and training to fit the skill profile of the jobs likely to be created …suggesting a shortage of up to 1.5 million workers with bachelor's degrees or higher in 2020…and nearly six million Americans without high school and college diplomas are likely to be without a job.

McKinsey Global Institute indicates that some of the problems stem from the mismatch between post-secondary education choices and the skill-sets required for employment:

> "Too few ... choose fields of study that will give the specific skills employers are seeking. Shortages (are projected) for nutritionists, welders, nurse's aides ... computer specialists and engineers."

The report from the McKinsey Inst. is specific in its appeal for policies and initiatives designed to develop the workforce of the future, not just produce graduates with general credentials. The researchers reiterate the theme that employers are not able to find employees with the skills required to fill available openings, in spite of rising levels of educational attainment in the U.S. and large investments by the federal government in education and workforce development.

The research also mentioned the "time" it takes to finish a degree along with many challenges students face that affect their ability to finish with appropriate qualifications. For example, in July 2013, I was asked to write a letter for a student returning to Miami Dade College in support of getting her financial aid re-established. The student had been in a domestic violence relationship and this affected her emotional and psychological state, preventing her from finishing the courses she originally signed up for. This student also lost her home and had her children removed from her custody. This situation is, unfortunately, typical of why some students are not finishing school.

Stagnant college completion rates are not the only problem. Students who drop out earn significantly less that those who graduate. Bridgeland, Milano, and Rosenblum (2011) described a survey that was conducted by Civic Enterprises and Hart Research with over 450 business leaders, 751 post-secondary leaders, community colleges, private sector career colleges and less selective four year institutions for their perspectives on challenges, goals, and work ahead to bridge the great divide. Here are some of their findings:

#1- **Most business leaders, (98 percent) believe the term "college" means a four-year degree. Just 13 percent of business leaders consider a two-year associate's degree to mean "college," and only 10 percent say "college" includes a career or technical credential**. By the end of this decade, just about an equal percentage of jobs will require a bachelor's degree or better (33 percent) some college or (30 percent) a two-year associate's degree.

#2- **Sixty-three percent (63 percent) of business leaders believe a four-year bachelor's degree is the primary degree to achieving success in the workplace, while only 18 percent believe a career or technical**

21

credential and 14 percent believe a two-year associate's degree are important to achieve such success.

#3- **Almost half (47 percent) of business leaders believe a four year bachelor's degree offers the best return on investment for their companies and for students. Thirty-five (35) percent felt the same way for career and vocational education. Only 18 percent of business leaders felt two-year associate's degrees offered a good return** on investment for students and only 15 percent believed such a degree was a good return on investment for their companies.

Business and education leaders see different priorities for postsecondary education based on their own missions:

#1- **The survey showed employers' focus on four-year degrees and place priority on career credentials in post-secondary education.** When asked to select the two most important goals for post-secondary education, 56 percent of business leaders placed the greatest premium on preparing individuals for success in the workplace. Providing individuals with core academic knowledge and skills rated 51 percent while providing individuals with the workforce knowledge and skills for success in a specific career rated 50 percent.

#2- **Highlighting the disconnect between classroom learning and the workplace, education leaders place greater emphasis on academic knowledge than career skills.** When asked to select the two most important goals for post-secondary education, educators placed the greatest premium on providing individuals with core academic knowledge and skills (64 percent), and preparing individuals to be lifelong learners (47 percent). Generally, preparing individuals for success in the workplace rated 44 percent. Just 28 percent of education leaders said providing individuals with the workforce knowledge and skills for success in a specific career was their single or second most important priority.

#3- **Community colleges can best serve their students by recognizing the market value and demand for career credentials.** When asked to rank the two most important goals for post-secondary education, nearly twice as many community college leaders selected providing individuals with core academic knowledge and intellectual skills (60 percent) than providing individuals with the workforce skills and knowledge for success in a specific career (34 percent).

The **financial gap** is another issue. Over 80 percent of education leaders that were surveyed identified students' financial pressures, such as needing to work, as a major challenge to their completing a post-secondary degree or credential at their institution. Bridgeland, Milano and Rosenblum, (2011) state, "Forty-two percent of education leaders selected their students' need to work as the single biggest obstacle to improving post-secondary completion rates at their institution." The gap seems to widen because college students practically live on credit cards and student loans. According to the College Board the average 2012-2013 tuition rose 4.2 percent in private colleges and 4.8 percent in public universities. "The ten year historical rate of increase is approximately six percent. These figures are substantially higher than the general inflation rate," according to Saving for College.com (2013).

According to a 2012 Well Fargo survey of 1,414 millennials between ages of 22 to 32, more than half financed their education through student loans. The Wells Fargo survey found that 79 percent of the millennials said that high schools and colleges should develop course curricula in basic investing, how loans work and saving for retirement during the first and last semesters. Even the Consumer Financial Protection Bureau found student debt affecting students' living arrangements. The Census data "reveals that nearly six million Americans ages 25-34 live with their parents."

It is also evident that college tuition is not only increasing but placing a strain on college students. Turl (2012) mentioned that many college students are still trying to make ends meet. I have two sisters who attend Miami Dade College and who were fortunate to be hired part-time at the college. They have not felt the full effect of recent recessions but this is not the case for many of our struggling students. National Public Radio (NPR) (2013) reported "for many college students and their families, rising tuition costs and a tough economy are presenting new challenges as college bills pour in." This has led to a little-known but important issue of college students facing hunger and sometimes homelessness. College presidents and leadership departments say more and more students are struggling. Michelle Asha Cooper of the Institute for Higher Education told a reporter that some are taking out large student loans to offset their living costs. Some are enrolling part-time, while others are even dropping out.

To combat this issue the University of California at Los Angeles (UCLA) created an "Economic Crisis Response Team" to help college students stay enrolled, graduate and hopefully join the workforce. To further assist in this matter, the National Association for the Education of Homeless Children and Youth provides scholarship assistance to students who are homeless or have experienced homelessness through the LeTendre Education Fund for Homeless Children and Young Adults.

THE PATHWAY FORWARD

The future lies before you. Like a field of driven snow, be careful
how you tread it, for every step will show. -- Author Unknown

Experts say the pathway forward consists of learning from experience and providing a clear roadmap to corporate success. The debate over the last 20 years has had to do with the whole notion of "skills" versus "knowledge." Humphrey (2011) states that the "assumption that knowledge is an academic acquisition, and it is somehow superior to skills is a misnomer." Frustrated employers who are not able to hire the talent they need have caused a chasm in our society because of the dichotomy of the "skills" versus "knowledge" philosophy. Business organizations must realize that those community colleges that offer two year degrees play a great role in creating a workforce equipped with both skills *and* knowledge. They have the ability to teach and train students in the necessary skill-sets they need to be more competitive.

Next, we need to bridge the gap by pulling the plug on college drop outs. Businesses have invested a great amount financially to retain workers but much more need to be done to reduce this epidemic, while at the same time making it more appealing for students to attain their degree. "To be the first in the world in educational attainment by the end of the decade, we must recognize the value of career credentials and associate's degrees; re-imagine how these degrees are offered; ensure they are more closely aligned with workforce needs; create incentive for students, post-secondary institution, and businesses to reward completion; and measure our efforts to ensure we are accountable for results" (Bridgeland, Milano and Rosenblum, 2011).

The article suggests the following to help reduce and eliminate the gap between young college workers and employers. The article reported the following to help close the gap:

(1) **Make Credentials Count**. Employers and especially smaller companies value credentials that show reliable career knowledge and skills. For this to happen, business leaders need to articulate what skills they need graduates to learn.

(2) **Foster Business and Community College Partnerships**. Collaborations between corporate America and learning institutions are vital to ensure that graduates have the desired competencies required by the business community. The successful "Earn to Learn" models outlined how partnerships could bring a balance to the collegiate and corporate communities. For example, UPS' partnership with Jefferson Community and Technical College, and The University of Louisville and Wal-Mart's partnership with American Public University all saw a remarkable difference with student graduation. South Florida Workforce has partnered with Florida International University's Pino Global Entrepreneurship Center (Pino Center) to implement and administer a Virtual Entrepreneurship Incubation Network (VEIN) a program that promotes business start-ups through virtual mentoring and entrepreneurial training.

(3) **Change the Vernacular**. The survey reveals that 98 percent of business leaders view "college" as only a four-year degree program; 13 percent include a two-year degree program to mean "college," and 10 percent say college conjures up thoughts of a career or technical credentials. Unfortunately what they fail to realize is that "while the majority of post-secondary students attend four-year institutions, nearly 40 percent of post-secondary students are enrolled in two-year institutions." Many of our students have the challenge of balancing work (some work 20-35 hours a week) and family life, along with college careers. The best way to ensure that the majority of workers contribute to the prosperity of this nation is to simply remove the chasm of two-year or four- year programs and just view "college" as college.

(4) **Get the Transfers Right**. Research from the United States Department of Education and National Center of Education Statistics (2010) reported that by increasing the number of students who graduate with associates' degrees we will see an economic boost and strong job growth in the coming decade. This certainly sounds promising. Since employers view a bachelor's degree as the highest return on their investment, "making transfer agreements more transparent, better structured and

tightly articulated to high-value bachelor's degree pathways is critical" (Bridgeland, Milano and Rosenblum, 2011).

(5) **Offer Incentive Completion, not just Enrollment**. Proponents stress the importance of giving students a reason to graduate. Now, this should be obvious, right? Sometimes it takes external motivating factors to give students a little push. An example of a good incentive is the *partial loan forgiveness* for students who persist and graduate, and I know many colleges/universities that have implemented this strategy. Another great incentive is *increases in Pell grant contributions* to enable students to progress through their coursework to earn their degree or credentials. A final incentive is the tax incentive for businesses to *reduce the cost of "Earn and Learn"* programs. Business leaders reported they were more likely to engage in "direct efforts to increase the number of post-secondary degree holders (such as tuition assistance programs, internships, partnerships with postsecondary institutions, etc.) if they were offered tax incentives to reduce the costs of participation." (Bridgeland, Milano and Rosenblum, 2011)

(6) **Measure Success and Failure**. The Students Right-to-Know (SRK) and Security Act (Public Law 101-542) of 1990 requires higher education institutions to report graduation rates to the National Center for Education Statistic (NCES) in order to receive financial aid. Although this sounds wonderful, the problem is that the numbers reported are rarely 100 percent accurate. The U.S. Department of Education Data System (IPEDS) states that the majority of students at public intuitions are *NOT* being tracked at all. So the information that is received cannot accurately depict the true success of the institution.

(7) **Offer Reward System to Motivate Students.** There needs to be a reward system in place to motivate college students to complete their degrees. There needs to be a better marriage between the idea of "access" and "completion." Bridgeland et al. (2011) suggest that higher level institutions and businesses need to examine and re-align incentives to ensure that students, post-secondary institutions, and employers focus on "rewards" to help increase graduation rates (Marcus, 2013).

While enrolling more students may increase an institution's budget, graduating students are rarely taken into consideration even though it is the goal of higher education institutions. This kind of budgeting, divorced from performance, does not give institutions any strong incentive to improve their completion rates, says Bridgeland, Milano and Rosenblum, (2011). Rewarding students for completing can provide a great boost in college completion particularly in lower income students who are less likely to finish without financial help. "Financial aid policies can be structured to incentivize finishing college course while still in high school, completing full college loads and earning degrees and certifications. Incentivizing off-peak registration (to maximize use of educational institution space) are other ways to foster completion through financial aid programs" (College Productivity, 2012).

Many states are addressing this issue and providing incentives for students to graduate. Below is a list of key states that are working feverishly to financially motivate students to finish their degrees.

LOUISIANA's *Opening Doors* scholarship program (cut short by Hurricane Katrina) incentivized completion, with an eye on low-income students. Students were found more likely to register full-time and stay in school at least four semesters.

OKLAHOMA adopted a program called *Oklahoma's Promise* that offers high school students with family incomes below $50,000 scholarships toward higher education. A five-year expiration date rounds out the incentive to enroll full-time and complete a degree.

FLORIDA required recipients of its *Bright Futures* merit scholarship to refund money if they dropped courses after the drop/add deadline. The result? A 50 percent reduction in dropped courses and $15 million in savings.

TEXAS has tested and launched numerous incentives, including the *College for All Texans $1,000 Tuition Rebate*, which allows students to graduate with a streamlined number of credits. In 2013, Thomas Melecki, director of student services, said the University of Texas launched a pilot program for freshman students that pays off a portion of their federal National Direct Unsubsidized Loans—which have an annual interest rate of 6.8 percent—if students meet certain guidelines. Students must complete 15 credit hours per semester; by the end of four years this could be a savings of over $12,975.

OHIO has what's called a *carrot and stick* approach to getting students to graduate. Farkas (2012) states the "carrot" could be in the form of incentives like tuition rebates and loan forgiveness for those who graduate in four years with an acceptable grade point average. The "stick" might be imposed additional fees and cost on students who take too long to earn their degrees.

The *Complete College Ohio Task Force* (2012) offered other suggestions to motivate students to complete their degrees. Below are some suggestions:

- Establish a "contract" between the student and the university that would lock in tuition if the student attains a degree within an agreed-upon time frame.
- Increase tuition to the out-of-state rate for any student still taking courses after accruing credit hours well beyond what is needed for graduation.

- Increase financial aid as students near completion or hold some back if they lag behind.
- Offer scholarships or financial aid if a student maintains a specific grade point average.
- Offer "stepping stone" grants and scholarships to a student who graduates from a community college and immediately transfers to a four-year institution.
- Establish a state or college program to provide financial assistance to students who enroll in summer courses.

COLLEGE SKILLS CONNECTION

"Habit is the intersection of knowledge (what to do), skill (how to do), and desire (want to do)."
- Stephen R. Covey, *The 7 Habits of Highly Effective People*

An Office of Employment Policy Research study (2006) discussed the importance of college students understanding what employers are looking for and how to remain competitive. The study further stated the essential skills to getting a job were still somewhat lacking in college graduates. In another survey, "*Are They Ready to Work? Employers Perspective on the Basic Knowledge and Applied Skills of New Entrants to the 21st Century U.S. Workforce*" (2006, p. 1.), college students might be in for a surprise as to what employers are really seeking.

Answering the key question, "What do employers look for in new employees?" were 461 business leaders. The survey was conducted by Corporate Voices for Working Families, Partnership for 21st Century Skills, and the Society for Human Resources Management. The report showed that although the three R's (reading, writing, and arithmetic) are still fundamental to every employee's success, employers now view "soft" skills as more important for gaining a competitive edge. The report listed four skills sets (ranging from minimal proficiency to some proficiency) young workers often lack. The list includes:

✓ Oral and written communication
✓ Professionalism and work ethic
✓ Teamwork and collaborative skills
✓ Critical thinking and problem-solving skills

Since this book is designed to increase your employment success, here are some tips to propel you forward. I have decided to focus on the four skill sets employers want in an ideal candidate:

(1) **Communication Skills are Essential**. The National Association of Colleges and Employers surveyed more than 200 employers about their top 10 priorities in new hires. Forty-four percent of responders cited soft skills, such as communication, critical thinking, creativity and collaboration as the areas with the biggest employment gap. It's imperative that college students pay close attention in the classroom, especially when asked to lead discussion groups or write scholarly essays. Once mastered, these skills catapult individuals into desired corporate settings. For instance, a supervisor might ask for your opinion about a new project or idea and wants you to express it in writing. You may be asked to provide a summary of a meeting or you may be asked to provide clear feedback on a report.

The annual global Talent Shortage Survey from Manpower Group reported 1 in 5 employers worldwide can't fill positions because they can't find people with soft skills and strong writing backgrounds. According to the article *"Communication Skills Key for Young Workers," Hastings (2012)* communication is the mode of choice in most workplaces today. "Being able to communicate in writing is critical to how far young workers are going to advance," according to Mark Bugaieski, SPHR, HR director for Illinois CancerCare. Whether someone is sending an e-mail or instant message or writing a blog, they are being judged on their communication ability, he said. "It must be good to attain success."

Listen the paper memo is dead, replaced by voicemail, informal conversations, e-mails and fax-mail. I also found out that there are two writing tasks that looms before the entry level workers: writing reports and filling out forms. For instance, many companies these days are seeking certification in a variety of world-class standard programs, like the International Standard Organization (ISO) or Quality Standard (QS) 9000, an automotive quality certification. The ISO 9000 family of quality management systems standards was designed to help organizations ensure they meet the needs of customers and stakeholders. QS9000 was a quality standard developed through a joint effort of the big three American automakers: General Motors, Chrysler, and Ford. For both of these programs, strong communication skills are paramount.

Furthermore, these certifications require extensive documentation. Workers have to complete reports that ask them to describe exactly what they do and how they do it. Proper grammar is essential to making an impact. If your writing is poor, do four things:

1. Read, read, and read excessively.
2. Always ask for an opinion on a document before you send it to your boss.
3. Always be familiar with who, what, when, where, how and why fundamentals.
4. When in doubt, use what I call "life notes;" this means you should refer back to your Bedford Handbook, grammar texts, websites or any resource to help you brush up on your grammar in order to remain at the top of your job performance.

A. On a scale of 1 to 5 (with 1 being the lowest, and 5 being highest), what is your communication (written and spoken) skill level? _____

B. Will they hire you? _____ If so, why? If not, why not? _____

C. Is there area for improvement? _____ Explain. _____

D. List four ways you plan to improve.
   a. _____
   b. _____
   c. _____
   d. _____

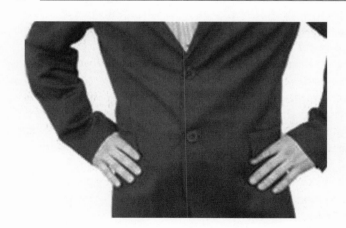

(2) **Professionalism is Essential to getting the Business Deal/Contract**. Did you know that more business transactions are taking place over dinner? Your nonverbal communication and verbal interactions can make or break you. The way you dress can also have a direct impact not only on whether you'll get hired, but also in keeping your job. Preparing for a job interview should always mean looking and dressing professionally.

While many major companies have adopted casual dressing, it's usually reserved for individuals who have already been hired; most companies still have a standard professional dress code. Casual dressing was introduced in the 1980s and early 1990s due to excessive layoffs. In her article "The Effect of Casual Dress on Performance in the Workplace," Hughes (2013) agrees with McPherson (2015, p. 134) when he stated, "The casual look was never meant to replace traditional Monday through Thursday business attire."

"Casual dressing was the result of two distinct trends: a return to elegance as a way of conveying professionalism, and a loosening up of formal dress codes, as demonstrated by casual Fridays and dress-down days" (Biecher, et al. 2015, p. 17). But honey wake up, the "business casual trend is NOT about fashion; it is about the whole casualization of America." However, in today's corporate arena you dress to impress.

Resume - Make sure that your resume and cover letter are also "dressed to impress" (see Chapter 4). Doing your research and knowing what the company's brand and future projects are make you look smart. Knowing about the business and demonstrating a strong work ethic go hand in hand.

Professional Demeanor - If you are a male student (regardless of cultural background), you can't speak slang, sag your pants, hold the crotch of your pants or wear a t-shirt to work, talk on your cell phone while you are on the clock, communicate in an unprofessional manner (i.e., using racially biased comments, off-color jokes, slang, foul words, etc.) like you do with your friends. If that's you, no way are you showing professionalism. You will never hold the job long and a career will be out of your reach.

If you are a female student (regardless of cultural background), you cannot dress provocatively, show cleavage, chew gum, wear hair styles that distract, communicate in an unprofessional manner, (i.e., using slang, foul words, avoiding eye contact, rambling, flirting, giggling too much, etc.) like you do with your friends. The constant texting and Facebooking, tweeting, video chatting during work time is a big no-no. You will be replaced immediately. Superiors will silently cross you off their "good" list. Avoid these pitfalls. Getting the job may be easy, but keeping it is another story. Professionals act, speak, and carry themselves with a corporate mindset. Money means nothing if your character and professional decorum are not intact.

A. On a scale of 1 to 5 (1 being the least and 5 being highest). How is your professional decorum? _____

B. Will they hire you? _____. Is there area for improvement? _____

C. List four ways you plan to improve.

a. _____

b. _____

c. _____

d. _____

(3) **Teamwork and Collaboration are Essential** and a natural part of life. Hughes & Jones (2013), in a 2009 poll conducted on behalf of the Association of American Colleges and Universities (AACU) posits, 71 percent of employers said they wanted colleges to place greater emphasis on "teamwork skills and the ability to collaborate with others in diverse group settings" (Hart, 2010, p. 2). The U.S. Air Force Academy requires teamwork in performance reviews, a skill endorsed by every officer. Strong teamwork collaboration can increase one's rank and seniority in the organization (O'Donnell, 2008). Coeling and Wilcox (2014) surveyed nurses and physicians to explore communication dimensions that impact collaboration. They focused on communication elements, including content (what is said), relationship styles (delivery of content and how the sender perceives the relationship with the other party), and time (amount of time needed for a good communication process to develop). Their analysis revealed that physicians and nurses place a high value on collaboration but different priorities on the communication elements. Students majoring in the healthcare profession should understand the importance of teamwork, especially since they must rely on fellow co-workers to help save patients' lives.

Many college students "hate" working in groups. In my speech classes, student normally put up a fight whenever it comes to group projects. I always explain to my students that my course is not just about giving presentations, it's about collaborative learning. In actuality, I bring Corporate America into the classroom to increase learning. What would you do if you worked with a colleague who didn't respond to emails on time? How would you feel if you had to make up the slack for their inadequate work? How quickly would you want to be on a team with someone whose work you had to revamp? Well, if you think teamwork in the classroom is a challenge, just wait until you enter the workforce. However, with every challenge comes a solution. In Corporate America working on a team allows you to build and establish relationships, develop trust, network, and share the workload. It also promotes healthy competition among co-workers to increase productivity.

A. On a scale of 1 to 5 (1 being the least and 5 being highest). How is your professional decorum? _____

B. Will they hire you? _____ Is there area for improvement? _____

C. List four ways you plan to improve.

a. _____

b. _____

c. _____

d. _____

(4) **Thinking Critically and Solving Problems** are vital for corporate success. In fact, Miami Dade College feel so strongly that students learn critical and creative thinking skills that they have incorporated as Outcome Three in MDC's Ten Learning Outcomes (TLO's) that graduates must fulfill.

The importance of critical thinking in *and* outside the classroom is vital. Since classical times, debates have been one of the best methods of learning and applying the principles of critical thinking. In fact, I designed a group debate assignment in my speech classes so that students can think and reason critically through debate, research, presentation and classroom activities. For instance, my speech classes studied the George Zimmerman trial in the Trayvon Martin murder case (2012-2013). They learned and were tested on their ability to argue viewpoints critically, clearly and factually. I also designed a short debate assignment where students had to argue and debate the topic: Stand Your Ground Law. Both sides had to argue for or against the law and using the Zimmerman case as evidence, a juror of six students had to determine the outcome. This meant students had to read and gather evidence, argue with sound reasons to support their claims, and articulate their findings in a persuasive manner to move the jurors to vote for the most effective team arguments. This assignment has become a norm in my class. Although college classrooms are trying to implement critical thinking projects and research, the level and depth may not be enough for future job success.

Taylor (2010) addresses a major concern from *The Wall Street Journal*'s survey of 479 college recruiters in which critical thinking skills, problem-solving skills and the ability to think independently were a major concern. In fact, Sara Holoubek, chief executive of Luminary Labs, a boutique consulting firm in New York, states the graduates she hires are bright "but can't seem to turn their isolated observations about the client's business into a strategy, despite the fact that they are often better observers than their superiors. This inability to assert an opinion holds young employees back..." Mildred Garcia, president of California State University, Fullerton and chair of AAC&U's board of directors, has said that "No matter what careers students seek, college education must equip them with intercultural skills, ethical judgment, and a sophisticated understanding of the diversity of our society and of any successful business or organization."

The Association of American College and Universities (AAC&U) (2013) released a report stating, "It takes more than just a major to reduce this gap. The survey, *Employer Priorities of College Learning and Students Success,* found 74 percent of business and nonprofit leaders recommend a 21st century liberal arts education. They emphasize the importance of being able to think critically and resolve problems in the corporate setting. "We need to raise the water table by improving the analytical skills, the critical thinking skills, the communication skills that are necessary for really almost every job in today's economy," said Green (2009).

According to Taylor (2010), many employers are trying to bridge the gap by:

1. Signing up recent graduates for external training.
2. Spending extra time developing independent and critical thinking skills in their new hires through simulated scenarios and role plays.
3. Launching the new Springboard Project, chaired by Accenture PLC Chairman and Chief Executive William D. Green. They have a free online video series called **JobsSTART 101**. The purpose of the project is "dot connecting skills."
A. On a scale of 1 to 5 (1 being the least and 5 being highest). How are your critical thinking and problem solving skills? _____
B. Will you be hired for the job? _____ Is there area for improvement? _____

    _____

C. List four ways you plan to improve.
    a. _____
    b. _____
    c. _____
    d. _____

WHAT EVERY COLLEGE STUDENT NEEDS TO KNOW

"No thief, however skillful, can rob one of knowledge, and that is why knowledge is the best and safest treasure to acquire" --L. Frank Baum

The research taken from the Hart Research Associates (2009) interview where 302 employers had to have at least 25 employees, 25 percent or more of them had to be new hires with associate degrees from a two-year college or bachelor's degrees from a four year college. The research suggested that employers want their employees *"to use a broader set of skills and have higher levels of learning and knowledge than in the past"* in order to meet the demand of an increasing complex workforce.

What Today's Employers Are Expecting From Recent Graduates

To complete a significant project before graduation that demonstrates their depth of knowledge in their major and their acquisition of analytical, problem-solving, and communication skills	62%
To complete an internship or community-based field project to connect classroom learning with real-world experiences	66%
To develop the skills to research questions in their field and develop evidence-based analyses	57%
To work through ethical issues and debates to form their own judgments about the issues at stake	48%
To acquire hands-on or direct experience with the methods of science so they will understand how scientific judgments are reached	40%
To learn about cultural and ethnic diversity in the context of the United States	34%
To learn about the point of view of societies other than those of Western Europe or North America	35%
To take courses that explore big challenges facing society, such as environmental sustainability, public health, or human rights	28%

Source: Hart Research Associates (2009)

The research confirms employer's support of learning outcomes necessary for student success in Corporate America. Employers endorse supportive practices that demonstrate the following:

a) Students' acquisition of both depth of knowledge in their major and broad skills,
b) Students' ability to apply their college learning in real-world settings, and
c) Students' development of ability to conduct research and develop evidence-based analysis (Harts 2009).

The research points out that employers believe colleges and universities should place greater emphasis on learning outcomes developed through a liberal education, which include the following:

Knowledge of Human Cultures/Physical and Natural World

Concepts and new developments in science and technology	70%
The ability to understand the global context of situations and decisions	67%
Global issues and developments and their implications for the future	65%
The role of the United States in the world	57%
Cultural diversity in America and other countries	57%

Intellectual and Practical Skills

The ability to communicate effectively, orally and in writing	89%
Critical thinking and analytical reasoning skills	81%
The ability to analyze and solve complex problems	75%
Teamwork skills and the ability to collaborate with others in diverse group settings	71%
The ability to innovate and be creative	70%
The ability to locate, organize, and evaluate information from multiple sources	68%
The ability to work with numbers and understand statistics	63%

Personal and Social Responsibility

The ability to connect choices and actions to ethical decisions	75%
Civic knowledge, civic participation, and community engagement	52%

Integrative Learning

The ability to apply knowledge and skills to real-world settings through internships or other hands-on experiences	79%

Source: Hart, 2009

THE FUTURE IN *S.T.E.M.* CAREERS

"... Leadership tomorrow depends on how we educate our students today—especially in science, technology, engineering and math."—
President Barack Obama, September 16, 2010

A STEM CAREER

I had a conversation with my son and daughter (6th and 7th graders) while writing this chapter. I asked them if they knew anything about STEM courses. They referred to a plant. I chuckled because they were correct, but that was not the answer I was looking for. Even though my children are young, I wanted them to be informed. I told them they should consider a future career in the STEM field, a clear pathway forward for connecting the necessary skills college students will need in today's demanding STEM job market. Students majoring in the STEM (science, technology, engineering and math) field are earning more money than non-STEM majors. So, why should one care about this career field? I can answer this question five ways (Refer to the section on page 46 for 10 reasons to pursue a STEM career).

The government is providing $3.1 billion in programs across the federal government to STEM education, an increase of 6.7 percent over 2012 funding (White House Office of Science & Technology, 2013). This is a major incentive for learning institutions to development curricula geared to STEM. This means your chances of securing financial aid may be higher due to the demand, and finding employment and connecting with the skills managers need is increasing rapidly. The U.S. Department of Commerce Economics and Statistics Administration (2011) states that STEM occupations are projected to grow by 17.0 percent from 2008 to 2018, compared to 9.8 percent growth for non-STEM occupations.

(1) **Increased STEM job growth**. Figures 1.1 & 1.4 (below) clearly show the job growth and by 2020 who will be looking for students majoring in the STEM field.

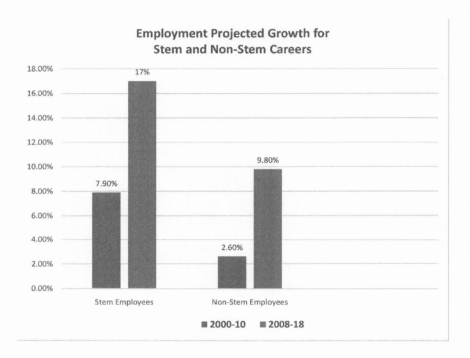

(2) **Better job satisfaction and security**, in Figure 1.2 (below)

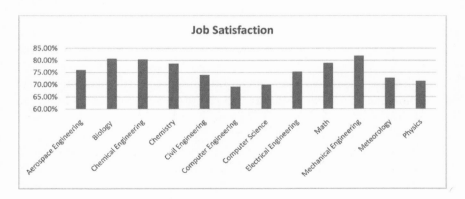

(3) **You earn more money**. In Figures 1.3 (below) salaries are higher among STEM careers than non-STEM. McCuistion (2013) states that a recent Georgetown study found that pay for those in STEM fields is high, and it continues to increase. People who major in STEM for undergraduate studies make nearly $500,000 more over their lifetime that non-STEM majors.

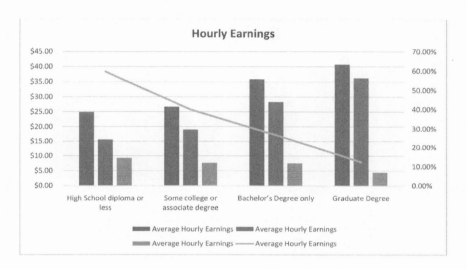

(4) **The STEM career field *IS* the future** (Figure 1.4). According to U.S. Department of Commerce Economics and Statistics Administration (2011), science, technology, engineering and mathematics (STEM) workers drive our nation's innovation and competitiveness. However, U.S. businesses frequently voice concerns over the supply and availability of STEM workers. Over the past 10 years, growth in STEM jobs was three times as fast as growth in non-STEM jobs. STEM workers play a key role in the sustained growth and stability of the U.S. economy, and are a critical component to helping the U.S. win the future. In the article "STEM Jobs Help America Win the Future," United States Commerce Secretary, Locke (2011) posits, "STEM workers are helping America win the future by generating new ideas, new companies and new industries."

The Obama Administration has made STEM education a priority. His agenda is simple, move our students to the top of the international pack in science and math. President Obama said, "*Initiatives like Race to the Top*" and "*Educate to Innovate*" campaign demonstrate my administration's ongoing efforts to making sure Americans learn the science and technology skills they need to fill jobs for the future."

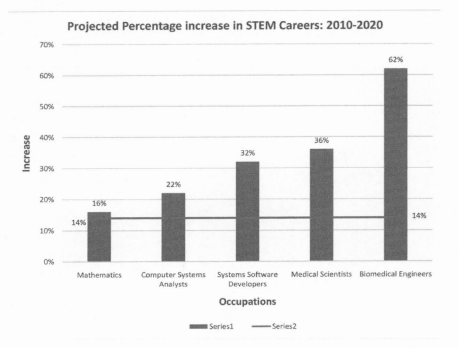

THE UNITED STATES PRESIDENT – LEARNING INSTITUTIONS & STEM

In February 2013, President Barack Obama stated, "We'll reward schools that develop new partnerships with colleges and employers and create classes that focus on science, technology, engineering, and math – the skills today's employers are looking for to fill jobs right now and in the future." This statement by the president is indicative of the changes that many schools and higher learning institutions are now undertaking. The Obama administration 2014 budget includes critical investments in a number of areas that will benefit aspiring students.

His administration is setting the foundation for the next 10 years. His budget calls for:

- **Recruiting, preparing and supporting excellent STEM teachers** with $80 million to support the President's goal of preparing $100,000 excellent STEM teachers and $35 million to launch a pilot STEM Master Teacher Corps.
- **Allocating an investment of $150 million to create new STEM Innovation Networks** to better connect schools districts with local, regional, and national resources.
- **Investing $300 million (from the Department of Education) to re-design schools to encourage partnerships** with colleges, employers and community partners focusing on high-demand employment in the STEM field.
- **Improving undergraduate STEM education.** The National Science Foundation (NSF) is launching a $123 million program to retain undergraduates in STEM fields.
- **Encouraging undergraduate teaching and learning in STEM subjects** to meet the President's goal of preparing one million more STEM graduates over the next decade
- **Promoting breakthrough research in STEM teaching and learning** with $65 million from Advanced Research Projects Agency for Education (ARPA-ED), which would allow the Department of Education to support high-risk, high-return research on next generation learning technologies, including STEM education.

COLLEGES/UNIVERSITIES BOOST STEM PROGRAMS

Students majoring in STEM career fields will have a major advantage over students who are not. Miami Dade College, Florida International University, University of Miami, University of Florida, Nova Southeastern University, and Barry University, just to name a few, along with other colleges and universities across the U.S. have tailored their academic programs to attract students majoring in the STEM career fields. For instance, a team of faculty members from Miami Dade College and the University of Florida won a five-year, $1.7 million federal grant to augment a distance education program which allows MDC students to earn a bachelor's degree in microbiology from UF. The grant was announced by the National Science Foundation (NSF) as a part of the STEM Talent Expansion Program.

The Biology Department at Miami Dade College, North Campus collaborates with Florida International University (FIU), St. Thomas University and Universidad Inter-Americana de Puerto Rico, San German, Puerto Rico in their STEM programs. Among other institutions, the Florida-Caribbean Consortium for Agriculture Education (FCCAgE) is partnering with Fairchild Tropical Botanical Garden and Earth Learning in order to offer students a holistic, multidisciplinary, and problem-based approach necessary for tackling tomorrow's agro-ecological challenges.

According to the Miami Dade College website, The Florida – Georgia Louis Stokes Alliance for Minority Participation (FGLSAMP) is poised to markedly increase the low participation of underrepresented minorities (URM) in science, technology, engineering, and mathematics (STEM) disciplines at the nine baccalaureate institutions that make up FGLSAMP. Since its inception in 1991, the alliance has experienced great success and STEM programs at alliance institutions have taken a lead role in reforming STEM undergraduate education and thus positively impacting our students. Comprised of 12 institutions within Florida and one in Georgia, the FGLSAMP institutional partners are Albany State University (ASU); Bethune-Cookman College (BCC); Florida International University (FIU); Florida Memorial University (FMC); Florida State University (FSU); University of Florida (UF); University of South Florida (USF); University of Central Florida (UCF University); University of Miami (UM); Tallahassee Community College (TCC); Miami Dade College (MDC); Florida Community College at Jacksonville (FCCJ); with Florida A&M University (FAMU) serving as the lead institution.

Spellman College has launched the Global Research and Education (G-STEM) to prepare African-American women within the STEM disciplines to be globally engaged upon their graduation from the college.

In 2012, Florida International University (FIU) launched the STEM Transformation Institute, a multidisciplinary partnership that has paved the way for student success in science, technology, engineering and math (STEM). Currently, FIU has approximately 7,500 undergraduates majoring in STEM and is considered the largest producer of STEM degrees for Hispanics. FIU also manages $20 million active STEM education grants, and has combined faculty from FIU's College of Arts & Science, College of Education, and College of Engineering and Computing to build a nationally recognized STEM education research group that will capitalize on their efforts and increase effective instructional techniques for the classroom.

NOVA Southeastern University Launched the Boy Scouts of America Science, Technology, Engineering and Math (STEM) Initiative. They developed a partnership with ExxonMobil which has an ongoing commitment to support a variety of collegiate programs to encourage an active interest in the STEM field by recruiting young students.

Florida State University (FSU) launched a summer camp for rising 8th through 12th graders, offering four major programs–FSU Teach; Science on the Move; Sea-to-Sea and SSTRIDE (Science Students Together Reaching Instructional Diversity & Excellence).

University of Miami (UM), Barry University, Florida Memorial University (FMC), and University of Florida (UF) are four of the 125 institutions and 12 university systems to join the Science and Mathematics Teacher Imperative (SMTI) initiative. In 2008, the Association of Public and Land-Grant Universities, funded in part by a $1.5 million grant from the National Science Foundation, launched a comprehensive package in mathematics and science to prepare students for success in higher education and beyond the classroom. The Science and Mathematics Teacher Imperative is the largest new-teacher initiative in the country. Through collaborative efforts in both state and national programs students will be able to compete on a global scale.

With all this being said you can see where the economy is headed and advancing in the next twenty years. So if you are looking to compete in the workforce, why not add the STEM track to your undergraduate program?

The Top 10 Reasons to Choose a STEM Career!

"Maintaining our leadership in research and technology is crucial to America's success ... if we want innovation to produce jobs in America and not overseas, then we also have to win the race to educate our kids." – President Barack Obama

The following has been adopted and revised from the Department of Educational Leadership and Policy Studies (2012).

THE TOP 10 REASONS TO CHOOSE A STEM MAJOR:

1. **Society**
   Science, Technology, Engineering and Mathematics (STEM) play a major role in our everyday life. Most likely, you read on your computer or access the Internet daily. You probably talk on a telephone or watch TV almost every day. Drive in a car that stops under a bridge or highway– all this is STEM. It is in everything we do! Being a part of developing and utilizing these tools is exciting and allows you to truly make a positive difference in the world.

2. **Fun**
   The world of STEM is constantly changing – breakthroughs are happening right this minute. With this transformative process your work is never dull. I believe you have to do what you love. When you love your work, you become the best worker in the world and you could never be paid enough because it goes beyond money. STEM offers the chance to pursue a career in something you will enjoy doing every day of your life.

3. **Flexibility**
   Since STEM is such a broad field, you have the freedom to choose from many specializations within each discipline; the possibilities are endless. It is impossible to predict what will happen next; therefore, no two days will be exactly the same. Variety is the spice of life, and STEM allows you to choose your own adventure.

4. **Challenge**
   If you enjoy doing puzzles, figuring out how an object works, understanding the wonders of the human body or creating new applications for world use, then a major in STEM may be just the right thing for you. In the ever-changing world of STEM you have to be able to adapt to new situations immediately. You have to scale hurdles, run through doors of possibilities, and yes, think "outside the box." Critical

46

thinking and reasoning skills are woven into your everyday life. This is all a part of the STEM field.

5. **Opportunity**

STEM majors are often referred to as the 'Swiss Army Knife' majors because of all the skills you acquire while studying them, leading to countless opportunities. STEM majors have many options available to them after finishing their undergraduate degree: attend graduate or professional school; work in a laboratory, for the government, or in the robotics field; conduct research; become a math or science teacher, or an actuary; or work as a legal analyst, lobbyist, or sector analyst, among many careers possibilities.

6. **Self and Career Satisfaction**

I feel sorry for the people who can't get genuinely excited about their work. Not only will they never be satisfied, but they also won' be completely fulfilled. Going to class and work every day should not be dreaded. Yes, there are going to be days when you may not want to get out of bed in the morning or you want to skip class, but the majority of the time, you should look forward to learning and growing. The Top 10 Careers for Happy Workers found that some of the most satisfying careers are in the STEM fields, like physical therapists, veterinary technicians, registered nurses, and engineers.

If you want to see how your desired profession measures up in job satisfaction, check out *JobsRated.com* to see the Top 200 most satisfying jobs based on stress, work environments, physical demands, income, outlook, and other measures of job satisfaction. Fifteen of the top 20 are from a branch of STEM, with the top four being actuary, software engineer, computer systems analyst, and biologist.

7. **Experiences**

Having a major in one of the STEM fields can bring about experiences that other majors might not be able to offer you. Recently, an article published by the *Wall Street Journal*, *"The Calculus Behind Buying Apple's iPhone 3G S"*, states that knowledge in STEM can help you navigate your everyday life in many different ways, from which cell phone to purchase to how to design a website. In fact, a STEM major can actually give you a leg up on the college experience because of the wide range of skills you will learn. Studying science, technology, engineering, and/or math may not be the simplest task you have ever done, but it will teach you a large set of skills right such as time management, organization, motivation, effective note-taking, and proper report writing.

8. **Motivation**

   Motivation is required in order to do anything, but that power can only come from within you. Goals can typically provide a direction for your motivation and help bring you success in a STEM major. It is important to have an end in sight. Right now, developing a "green economy" is one of the priorities in the U.S. If this is something to which you want to contribute, then consider a major/career in STEM. Motivation can come in many forms, such as a desire to invent something to help a family member manage a chronic illness, to find life on a distant planet, or to create the world's largest building. In order to attain these goals, you must find the motivation inside yourself. For more information on a "green economy," then check out this article, *Green Jobs: Toward Decent Work in a Sustainable, Low-Carbon World http://www.unep.org/PDF/ UNEPGreenjobs_report08.pdf*

9. **Geographic Mobility**

   Sometimes students in STEM are concerned about studying abroad during their undergraduate careers because they think they will fall behind in their classes; this is not the case at many schools. Actually, there is a program called the Trans-Atlantic Science Student Exchange Program (TASSEP). One of the benefits of a STEM major/career is that "even with different teaching styles, science is just science no matter where you go," says Matthew Van Wingerden, a student at the University of Washington.

   Miami Dade College offers students the opportunity to study abroad in six continents and over 30 countries. The college's *Consortium for International Studies* (CCIS) partnership with foreign institutions and The Confucius Institute has helped to provide a global perspective in in the Chinese culture. For this reason, many people enjoy the benefit of being able to travel and still speak the language of STEM.

10. **Money**

    STEM careers do encompass some of the fastest growing occupations, along with many of the highest paying occupations. For more information on these statistics and the career that you are interested in, go to *Career One Stop http://www.careeronestop.org/*. Also, keep in mind that it is not always about the money. As American businessman and investor Charles Schwab once said, "The man who does not work for the love of work, but only for money, is likely to neither make money nor find much fun in life." Remember his words as you go about pursuing your education and potential career. Do what you love, and love what you do.

APPENDIX

Table 2 *Detailed **STEM** & "**NON-STEM**" undergraduate majors*
The following table was taken from the U.S. Department of Commerce Economics and Statistics Administration.

Earth and Environmental Science	Physical Science
Aquaculture Manager	Astronomer
Aquarist	Audio and Video Equipment
Cartographers & Photogrammetrists	Technician
Climate Change Analyst *In Demand!*	Aviation Inspector
Diver	Chemical Technician
Emergency Management Specialist	Chemist
Environmental Compliance Inspector	Chemistry Teacher *In Demand!*
Environmental Scientist	Electrician *In Demand!*
Geographer *In Demand!*	Film and Video Editor
Geoscientist	Food Science Technician
Hydrologist	Food Scientist or Technologist
Industrial Health & Safety Engineer	Forensic Science Technician
Marine Architect	Nuclear Monitoring Technician
Meteorologist	Nuclear Power Reactor Operator
Soil and Water Conservationist	Occupational Health & Safety
Soil Scientist	Specialist
Surveyor	Physicist
System Operator	Physics Teacher *In Demand!*
Water & Liquid Waste Treatment	Pilot
Plant	Power Distributor & Dispatcher
Water or Wastewater Engineer *In*	Power Plant Operator
Demand!	Precision Instrument & Equipment
Technologist-*In Demand*	Repairer
Weatherization Installer or	Ship & Boat Captain
Technician *In Demand!*	Sound Engineering Technician
Wind Energy Engineer *In Demand!*	
Wind Turbine Service Technician	

Math & Computer Science	
Actuary	Mathematician
Computer Hardware Engineer	Multimedia Artist or Animator
Computer Programmer *In Demand!*	Network Systems & Data
Computer Software Engineer *In Demand!*	Communications Analyst
Database Administrator *In Demand!*	Remote Sensing Scientist or Technologist *In Demand!*
Economist	Software Quality Assurance Engineer & Tester
Math Teacher *In Demand!*	Statistician

Life Science

Agricultural Inspector
Agricultural Technician
Animal Breeder
Animal Trainer
Anthropologist
Athletic Trainer *In Demand!*
Audiologist *In Demand!*
Biochemist *In Demand!*
Bioinformatics Scientist *In Demand!*
Biological Technician
Biologist
Biology Teacher *In Demand!*
Biomedical Engineer *In Demand!*
Cardiovascular Technologist or
Technician *In Demand!*
Certified Registered Nurse
Anesthetist (CRNA) *In Demand!*
Chiropractor
Cytogenetic Technologist *In Demand!*
Cytotechnologist *In Demand!*
Dental Hygienist *In Demand!*
Dietitian or Nutritionist
Emergency Medical Technicians &
Paramedic *In Demand!*
Epidemiologist
Genetic Counselor
Health Educator *In Demand!*
Marine Biologist
Medical & Clinical Laboratory
Technician
Microbiologist
Registered Nurse *In Demand!*
Respiratory Therapist
Speech-Language Pathologist

Veterinarian *In Demand!*
Veterinary Technologist &
Technician *In Demand!*
Zoologist and Wildlife Biologist
Natural Sciences Manager
Neurologist *In Demand!*
Nuclear Medicine Technologist
Occupational Therapist *In Demand!*
Optometrist *In Demand!*
Pathologist *In Demand!*
Pharmacist *In Demand!*
Physical Therapist *In Demand!*
Physician
Physician Assistant *In Demand!*
Plant Scientist

Behavioral and Social Science

Marriage & Family Therapist *In Demand!*
Medical Social Worker *In Demand!*
Political Scientist
Psychologist
Sociologist

Interdisciplinary Science

Patent Lawyer *In Demand!*
Science Writer
Technical Writer

Engineering

Aerospace Engineer
Aerospace Engineering & Operations Technician
Architect
Automotive Engineer *In Demand!*
Biochemical Engineer *In Demand!*
Biofuel or Biodiesel Technology & Product Development Manager *In Demand!*
CAD Technician
Chemical Engineer
Civil Engineering Technician
Civil Engineers *In Demand!*
Commercial & Industrial Designer
Electrical & Electronics Engineer
Electrical Engineering Technician
Energy Engineer *In Demand!*
Environmental Engineer
Environmental Engineering Technician
Fuel Cell Engineer *In Demand!*
Geographic Information Systems Technician *In Demand!*
Hydroelectric Plant Technician
Industrial Engineer
Landscape Architect
Mapping Technician

Materials Scientist and Engineer
Mechanical Engineer
Microsystems Engineer *In Demand!*
Nano systems Engineer *In Demand!*
Nuclear Engineer
Petroleum Engineer
Photonics Engineer *In Demand!*
Photonics Technician *In Demand!*
Robotics Engineer *In Demand!*
Robotics Technician *In Demand!*
Semiconductor Processor
Solar Energy Systems Engineer *In Demand!*
Solar Photovoltaic Installer
Sustainability Specialist *In Demand!*
Technologist-*In Demand*
Transportation Engineer *In Demand!*
Transportation Planner *In Demand!*

Human Biology and Health	Medical & Clinical Laboratory Technician
	Medical Social Worker *In Demand!*
Biomedical Engineer *In Demand!*	Neurologist *In Demand!*
Cardiovascular Technologist or Technician *In Demand!*	Nuclear Medicine Technologist
Certified Registered Nurse Anesthetist (CRNA) *In Demand!*	Occupational Therapist *In Demand!*
	Optometrist *In Demand!*
Chiropractor	Pathologist *In Demand!*
Cytotechnologist *In Demand!*	Pharmacist *In Demand!*
Dental Hygienist *In Demand!*	Physical Therapist *In Demand!*
Emergency Medical Technicians & Paramedic *In Demand!*	Physician
	Physician Assistant *In Demand!*
Epidemiologist	Registered Nurse
Health Educator *In Demand!*	Respiratory Therapist

DISCOVER 9 COLLEGE MAJORS FOR THE FUTURE

"The future may be unknown but the fun part is discovery." --
K. Sterling-Hamilton

One of scariest things for a student is to graduate, only to find out that their career field is *not* in high demand. I know you're thinking; isn't that what college advisors are for? No, darling! They help students connect with their future by helping students clarify their educational goals and guiding them to academic success. Unfortunately, advisors are *not* required to know the intricate details and trends in the job market. Gearon (2012) researched nine top jobs for college graduates. His research was motivated by the workplace demand on higher level institutions to produce quality graduates to work in selected career fields. The following nine jobs are emerging career fields that are on the rise, as reported by the U.S. Bureau of Labor and Statistics.

1. **Biomedical Engineering.** This field combines engineering, science, and technology to discover innovative ways to heal the body. Our bodies go through so much wear and tear, so newly hired graduates in this field will help to invent or redesign devices, upgrade prosthetics, and even create robots to assist with surgeries. They will research and engineer new drugs and vaccines, and much more. The U.S. Bureau of Labor Statistics says this is the fastest-growing career field, with an expected 72 percent rate of job growth from 2012-2108. According to the Biomedical Engineering Accreditation Body, there are 64 undergraduate biomedical engineering programs around the country, and Miami Dade College implemented one in fall 2013. The University of Washington and Ohio State University have rolled out programs. There are several schools with established majors in this field, like Johns Hopkins University, Duke University, Georgia Institute of Technology, Massachusetts Institute of Technology, and University of California—San Diego.

2. **Computer Game Design**. There are three main career paths within the game industry; graduates can find positions as programmers, artists, or producers. According to a recent study this industry is expected to reach $82.4 billion globally, compared to $55.5 billion in 2010 (EdSource, 2013). Miami Dade is one college that is spearheading study programs in computer game design, where students can earn an AA in Computer Arts Animation that transfers to a BFA in computer animation or multimedia studies at any state university. Other institutions leading the way are

Becker College, Worcester Polytechnic Institute, DePaul University, Michigan State University and Rochester Institute of Technology.

3. **Environmental Studies/Sustainability.** This area is extremely significant to preserving humanity. This new area of study, which has emerged in the 21st century as a new academic discipline, was first introduced at the World Congress "Challenges in a Changing Earth Summit." The Sustainability Graduate Science Program at Harvard University outlined the development of sustainability science which seeks to advance basic understanding of the dynamics of human environment systems; facilitate the design, implementation and evaluation of practical interventions that promote sustainability in particular places and contexts; and improve linkages between relevant research and innovative communities (Kates, 2010)

Miami Dade College's Earth Ethics Institute began in 1993 and has now collaborated with Florida International University to develop a strategic alliance program, titled "Certificate in Agroecology," along with some 35 other institutions. Miami Dade College has taken the lead role to incorporate sustainability in class curriculum, workshops, symposiums, degrees, and certificates. Students at the University of Wisconsin—Madison can now major in either environmental studies or environmental sciences. Related fields of sustainability with a concentration in biological systems have also increased in popularity. Colleges such as Arizona State University, Pennsylvania State University, University of Kentucky and University of Oklahoma offer a bachelor's degree in this emerging major, according to the Association for the Advancement of Sustainability in Higher Education.

4. **Health Informatics/Information Management.** This particular career field is expected to increase by 21 percent from 2010-2020 *(Occupational Outlook Handbook 2012-2013)*. The demand for a variety of health services will increase due to an aging population, who will need more testing, treatments, and procedures. The transition to electronic technology in the health care field is gaining momentum. In 2011 the federal government implemented the Health Insurance Portability and Accountability Act (HIPAA), designed to secure personal information and protect patients' rights. This shift has created many new positions in health informatics. "The healthcare industry needs a workforce prepared to use the next generation health informatics technology" (Rodrigues, 2011).

According to the Commission on Accreditation of Health Informatics and Information Management Education, 54 baccalaureate programs in this field are currently accredited, including those at University of

Washington, Temple University, the University of Illinois—Chicago, and Weber State University. Heather Hodgson, a recent graduate from the College of St. Scholastica, stated, "This is a good path for someone who is not all about direct patient contact" but still wants to contribute to the health care field. Miami Dade College started a Health Informatics Certificate Program at the Medical Campus in 2011.

5. **Homeland Security.** Ever since the 9/11 attacks, America has changed. We witnessed the most devastating attack on U.S. soil. In his article, "How Border Security Has Changed Since 911," Flynn (2011) quoted U.S. Customs and Border Protection Chief Officer Agent Randy Gallegos who said, "Prior to 9/11 the Department of Homeland Security did not exist." As a result of the aftermath the Border Patrol Department was fully mobilized within 36 hours of the attacks. Supinski (2002), a director of partnership programs for the Naval Postgraduate School's Center for Homeland Defense and Security, says this career field is among the fastest-growing educational disciplines.

   More than 300 programs have sprouted since 9/11 and about 75 of these programs have led to undergraduate degrees, like The Naval Postgraduate Center which was created in 2002. Schools partnering with the center include Tulane University, Eastern Kentucky University, Texas A&M University, Florida International University, Monmouth University, and Endicott College. Meanwhile several universities are now offering bachelor's degrees in this career field; among them are Marian University, Tulane University, and Virginia Commonwealth University. Courses offered by many schools include critical infrastructure, criminal justice, emergency and disaster planning, and weapons and mass destruction just to name a few. Effective fall 2013, Miami Dade College implemented the Homeland Security Certificate Program.

6. **Information Assurance/Cyber Security.** There is a great demand in this field. It has grown tenfold over the last ten years (George, 2010). In this career field students learn about the technical aspects of protecting computer systems and networks. They also acquire knowledge in protecting computers systems from viruses, worms, hackers, terrorist threats and corporate espionage, just to name a few. National Aeronautic Space Administration (NASA) and the Department of Homeland Security sponsor the National Centers of Academic Excellence in Information Assurance, which "designates schools that meet established standards in teaching students to spot and fix vulnerabilities in the nation's information infrastructure" (George, 2010). Universities such as Mississippi State University, the University of Tulsa, Dartmouth College,

and Carnegie Mellon University are among the 66 institutions with undergraduate programs in this field.

7. **Nanotechnology.** Gearon (2011) says this industry is poised to grow to $2.4 trillion worldwide by 2015 and employ two million people in the U.S. by 2012. Listen, if you enjoy science, physics or anything in the microscopic realm you must consider this field. Since the future is at hand why not pursue a career that already is doing the following: making gold clubs, skis, car parts or stronger implants for dental users. I believe this field is the key to more-energy efficient fuel cells, solar panels, batteries, and environmental cleanup. The degrees prepare students for graduate school and careers in the health sciences field, as well as many others. The University at Albany started its program in 2004, and by 2010 had rolled out two new undergraduate degrees. Other institutions such as Drexel University, Louisiana Tech University, and University of Central Florida are on a similar track.

8. **New Media.** Everything is changing at the speed of light. This field is combining the old with the new. That's right. The combination of traditional journalism or communication studies and digital media and design is like a piece of pie made in heaven. New media can lead to jobs in filmmaking, television, game design, animation, graphic design, social media, and the list goes on. Institutions such as University of Southern California, Syracuse University, Wellesley College, and University of Minnesota offer programs of study in this career track.

9. **Public Health.** This career field taking the world by storm. This area is for students who have a passion to help prevent diseases and other health-related issues. If you like to research and spearhead intervention strategies at an early point to reduce consequences to the community, then this may be your calling. So exploring public health threats, whether they start at home or abroad, are chronic or acute, are curable or preventable, or are the result of human error deliberate or not, this major prepares students for entry-level positions in government agencies, health corporations, community nonprofit organizations and a host of healthcare facilities. Miami Dade College's School of Health Sciences provide several programs for students interested in this field. Other institutions such as University of Washington, East Tennessee State University, Tulane University, San Diego State University, University of California-Berkeley, University of Maryland, University of Miami, Johns Hopkins, and University of South Florida offer programs of study in this career track as well.

FUTURE BUSINESS PATHWAY

WHAT BUSINESS GRADUATES NEED TO KNOW

In the article "Six Business Skills Every New Graduate Needs to Develop," author Lester (2012), says in order for college students to be competitive there are six essential jobs skills necessary for success in the workforce, including the following.

HUMAN RELATIONS SKILLS

Human relations skills are invaluable, no matter what your job entails. Here are three you will want to develop to remain sharp.

(1) **Public Speaking:** When you graduate from an upper level institution you are expected to speak well. However this isn't the case for most college graduates. I teach public speaking and I remember during a class session I noticed one of my students struggling to read, write and articulate. So I ask him if he spoke Creole mostly at home. His response was, "Yes". This is the source of his problem. He was not speaking English enough and failed to complete the reading assignment in order to empower himself. Whether you are Jewish, Spanish, Haitian, Chinese, from Earth or Mars etc…you must speak the language of the dominant cultural in which you reside.

"Too many recent graduates are not equipped to present the company they work for properly, be it over the phone, in person or at networking events…," says Graham Chapman (2011), account coordinator/new business director at 919 Marketing, a PR and marketing firm in Holly

Springs, North Carolina. "If you can't speak [or] present yourself well, it is hard to help a company drive business. So look for volunteer activities where you can practice public speaking in front of small groups. Be willing to enlarge your scope to better yourself.

(2) **Handling Tense Interactions:** "Tension-filled conversations" go hand-in-hand with some of the work we do. Unfortunately, those who lack the ability to handle them effectively will have a difficult time," says Kerry Patterson (2003), co-author of Crucial Conversations.

Always get a proper assessment from those who observed the situation first. Try not to evaluate a situation based on emotions. Our emotions can create a train wreck. Rather try having an open honest dialogue and maintain proper office etiquette. If you find yourself in the middle of an intense situation it's best to remove yourself. Document the situation right away and report it immediately. Cover yourself at all times. In an intense situation you do your part to maintain peace. No one wants to work in an uncomfortable environment. It affects work productivity.

(3) **Teamwork:** "The reality of working with a team, where colleagues have a variety of thoughts and ideas that need to be respected, is often new to grads," says Bettina Seidman (2001), founder of Seidbet Associates, a career-management firm in New York City. Whenever I announce to my students they have to work together on a group project the classroom environment changes immediately. I hear, "Professor can I work alone?" "Is this going to be a group grade?" "How long do we have to work together?" "What if I don't want to work with a group?" My students are not particularly fond of the idea to group/teamwork. I try to impress upon them that no one is an island they need the assistance of others. Teamwork skills are critical to working environment. "The downside of not having these skills can be very serious, including gaining a poor reputation on the job, and even termination." So listen, listen, listen. Try to connect with someone that's seasoned and learn as much as you can. Be open and willing to work with others. This can only empower you.

CAREER-MANAGEMENT SKILLS

The following career-management skills will help you land your first job and position yourself for a promotion.

(4) **Humility and Patience:** Remember the race between the tortoise and rabbit. You would have thought the rabbit had it in the bag, but he didn't. He was cocky, arrogant, no discipline and in the end lost the race. Poor rabbit! I hope you are not that rabbit. Rulis (2011), a senior recruiter in

Western Union's talent acquisition group, exclaimed, "Managers want to promote individuals who are willing to prove themselves versus those who expect things to be handed to them right from the start." The tortoise may have been slow but he was focus on the goal. Humility and patience walks hand and hand. So take your time and learn the ropes. No one is an overnight success. "In most instances, you will learn how other leaders had to roll up their sleeves and prove themselves just like everyone else."

(5) **Staying Informed:** We say this often, "information is paramount". Professors don't emphasize the importance of reading the news, says Tom Gimbel (2010), CEO of The LaSalle Network, a Chicago-area professional staffing and recruiting firm. You look so impressive to managers when you can communicate the current happenings and be able to apply critical thinking as it relates to the current job market. "After a new grad has secured the job, emailing news stories or cutting out newspaper articles for their boss is beyond impressive." Read, read, read. The more you are aware of changes in your career field you become more marketable.

(6) **Time Management:** So you have successfully gone through the interview because you followed all the tips in chapter 3 of this book and you get hired. Congratulations! You are hanging with the big boys now; however, you seem to be getting stretched and don't know what to do. Your job duties are increasing and you're feeling a tad bit overwhelmed. "A new grad may feel obligated to say 'yes' to everything, which makes it even more difficult to manage their time," says Susan Fletcher (2010), psychologist and a time-management expert with Smart Zone Solutions in Plano, Texas. You may end up neglecting core activities or stretching yourself to the breaking point, she says. Time-management skills involve managing your energy and attention. Learn what to prioritize first. So put first things first. "Be intentional about what you commit to," Fletcher says. Ask for assistance when you have too. I would apply the 80/20 rule here. 80 percent of the work in 20 percent of the time because you included others who are more seasoned in the company who could help you navigate this challenging time until you get your balance.

MISTAKES COLLEGE GRADUATES MAKE WHEN SEEKING JOBS

"When it comes to the future, there are three kind of people: Those who let it happen, those who make it happen, and those who wonder what happened." -- John M. Richardson

A report from a March 2013 survey conducted by career website After College.com with 600 college students reported that 79 percent of respondents had completed at least one internship in the past six months. However, 57 percent of those internships were unpaid and 76 percent did not result in a job offer. So, what seems to be the problem? Here are five things I believe you need to consider when applying for a job.

1. **Students are *not* applying for enough jobs**. Okay, let me pause and ask you, how many jobs have *you* applied for over the past month? The survey found that 44 percent of students only apply for between 1-5 jobs at a time. Schawbel (2012) maintains that "students should go after 30-40 jobs at once. It's like a full-time job," he added. When you apply for more than one job you are able to negotiate better, especially if you have promising job offers. Now, applying for as many jobs as possible is a good idea; however, remember you have to do the research to make sure you are competent enough to *ACE* the job interviews. (Check out Chapter 3 for tips on how to answer key interview questions in corporate America.)

2. **Failing to Network**. Dictionary.com defines networking as a "supportive system of sharing information and services among individuals and groups that have a common interest." Fifty-one percent of the students

commented they wished their schools had offered more networking opportunities. Miami Dade College, Florida International University, Nova Southeastern University, Barry University and University of Miami offer a plethora of networking opportunities. For instance, University of Miami has the Engineers without Boarders Program and Miami Dade College offers service learning opportunities with over 350 non-profit organizations in our community. I encourage my students provide a certain amount of service learning hours each academic semester to help network and build their resumes.

Schawbel (2012) says, "The most valuable thing students can get from school career services is connections to alumni in their desired line of work". Alumni can teach students about the day-to-day realities of a job, how to craft a resume, how to interview and how to land a position. Stay in touch with professors, teachers and ask for tips to help you get in. I am constantly writing letters of references for students who keep in contact with me. In fact, as I am writing this chapter I am in the process of writing several letters of references. I also suggest you go to conferences and industry events. One event-listings site Schawbel recommends: *eventbright.com,* I also have to add the fact that you are reading this book puts you one step closer to your dream career.

3. **Facebooking and YouTubing when they should be LinkedIn.** The survey revealed that 90 percent of the students use Facebook, 78 percent regularly use YouTube; however only 46 percent reported using LinkedIn. So what's the fuss about LinkedIn, right? Why is this social networking site so important? Here are simple answers to these simple questions; it is a *professional* site for individuals in *professional* occupations and organization. It is **not** like Facebook. Scholars suggest that students need to create a LinkedIn profile during their freshmen year.

4. **The Mistaken Belief in applying *only* through an employer's website.** The survey found that 70 percent students first applied to the employer's website; however you can't just depend on the fact that although you submitted you information to the website that it would be enough. You must use a variety of follow-up mean to get notice and get called in for an interview. Turner (2014) suggested never call human resources or an in-house recruiter. These people have no vested interest in talking with you. In fact, they don't want to talk to you. You'll only foul up their process. If you want to get hired, you need to talk with an actual hiring manager. Find out who this person is before you send your resume anywhere. You can locate the names of these people through various sources such as the company Website's "About Us/Management Team" page, phoning

the company receptionist, or subscribing to a corporate research service like Hoovers, ThomasNet or Lead411.

5. **Taking *no* for an answer when the employer is unresponsive.** You had a great interview for the job. Your answers were spot on and you could feel the energy and synergy during your panel or one-on-one interview. However, it's been three weeks and you haven't heard from the employer. Just what could have happened? Nearly 49 percent of students say that companies never get back to them after they send in their resume or interview for a job. Listen, you cannot afford to just accept what's being handed to you. You are competing with hundreds, maybe thousands of individuals for the same interview. Here is what Schawbel recommends: visit your college career office, connect with your personal network of family and friends, use Facebook and LinkedIn and find that personal link. ***Do not*** give up if you don't get a call back.

6. **Forgetting to send a thank you letter.** I recall when trying desperately to get an interview at Miami Dade College, I called at least twice a week for about six months. They knew me by name. The moment I opened my mouth, someone would say, "Is this Katrika?" I was assertive. I was finally called in and though I went through four levels of interviews, I didn't hear from them. My aunt reminded me to send a thank you letter to seal the deal. I was hesitant at first, but was elated when I received a call the same day I provided the thank you letter, and was told, "You have been hired at Miami Dade College to work in our Speech Department." Thank God I listened to wisdom, and guess what? It worked; I got hired and so will you!

HOW TO STAND OUT

"Fitting in is easy, standing out takes courage." -- K. Sterling-Hamilton

CONSTANT FIRST IMPRESSIONS:

How you present yourself to others in the business world speaks volumes. Finish the sentence "I only have one time to make a _____". Yes, first impression! People often form first impressions about others within seconds after their initial meeting, so remember it is crucial to ensure you are properly prepared to present yourself as a professional. Here are some important tips towards making a good impression.

- Poise is important so stand straight and focus on who you are speaking to. People love when you give them good eye contact (this varies according to culture of course). Don't forget to smile and give your face a rest. A warm smile breaks the ice.
- Dress to impress. Whatever the dress code stipulates—do it. Follow the dress attire that the corporation demands.
- Meeting someone for the first time can create anxiety so go to your comfort zone (it's a mental projection of where you like to distress or who you enjoy being around.) Have that professional approach, firmly shake the persons hand because it communicates confidence (this varies according to culture of course so do your homework).

COMMUNICATION:

It's not what we say but how we say it and what we do that counts!

- Return phone calls and emails within 24 hours
- Some people are picky so get their permission to put them on speakerphone.
- Emails at work should be grammatically correct and free of spelling errors. Don't write using codes as if you're speaking to your friends. Your emails discloses how well you speak and what others will think about you
- Re-read your information several times especially if your content is tailored to your boss.

MEETINGS:

It doesn't matter where you work, be ready for constant meetings. Some meetings are informal or formal. Whether face to face or with a group of distinguished colleagues, the key is to maintain your professional edge at all times in this environment.

- For a meeting in someone's office, don't arrive more than five minutes early, as they may be prepping for your meeting, another meeting later that day, or trying to get other work done. You may make them uncomfortable, and that is not a good way to begin your meeting.
- Don't arrive late...ever. If you are going to be late, try to let someone know so that people are not sitting around waiting for you. Don't forget that being on time for a meeting means arriving 5 minutes early - for an interview, arrive 10 minutes early.
- Do not interrupt people. This is a bad habit to start and a tough one to end. Columbia University Center for Career Education (2013).

WORK SPACE ENVIRONMENT:

You may spend more waking hours in work spaces than in your home space so:

- Keep the space professional and neat with appropriate personal touches! Your office reflects you personally.
- Whether it is a cubicle or office, respect others' space. Don't barge in their office, knock first.

- Don't assume acknowledgement of your presence is an invitation to sit down; wait until you are invited to do so.
- Don't over talk anyone the polite thing to do is wait for their signal. So, if you have to stand there like a manikin until they give you clearance to communicate with them—do so. Read their non-verbal signals it just might not be the ideal time to conduct business.
- Don't interrupt people on the phone, and don't try to communicate with them verbally or with sign language. You could blow an important phone call.

GLOBAL BUSINESS ETIQUETTE:

As the global market grows, the need to understand multiple international standards of business etiquette grows. There are, however, a few key things to keep in mind when conducting business internationally:

- I can't say this enough you *MUST* do your homework when it comes to business etiquette and netiquette. Note take proper protocols, customs and follow them.
- Cultural diversity is a norm and knowing the language makes an excellent impression on the people you are doing business with. Use a dictionary to help you speak the language. Consider taking a class to help refine your intercultural communication skills.
- Time zones are important. Business deals can be affected because a person didn't pay attention to the time a project was due. This can ultimately lead to losing revenues and future business contracts. You also have to understand the importance of deadlines when it comes to time zones. Finding balance is important and completing tasks way ahead of schedule "if possible" is always a plus.
- As there is no standard global work day, you should keep in mind that work hours vary from country to country.
- Meals can be extremely crucial in making a positive international business etiquette impression. The customs that are followed when dining are often very important, and mistakes in this area could be costly! *Columbia University Center for Career Education (2013).*

Chapter 3

SAY IT LIKE THIS!

"If you say it like this, you will get hired like that!" -- K. Sterling-Hamilton

Ask any business owner and they will tell you that one of the most imperative goals of the business is to move products off the shelves into buyer's hands. My goal in this chapter is very similar; that is, to move you from the college classroom to your corporate desk.

You Are a Product!

First of all, you are the **product**. Why? Because you are always on display! Let's face it, when you see something you like, your first instinct is to stop, right? Why? So you can get a closer look. Similarly, after reading this chapter, you will become so sharpened that once you market yourself you will be sought out. Companies will want to get a closer look at *you* not just on paper but in person, meaning your interview and resume (view chapter 4) will help to catapult you into your dream career.

So, what is your product? Webster's Dictionary (2013) defines product as "an article or substance that is manufactured or refined for sale." You are that quality product that is up for sale. You are that product that needs to be moved from off the shelves into gainful employment. As you research your career field, you will find that the job market is like trying to find a needle in a haystack. Halimuddin (2013) says that only 42 percent of recent college graduates are working in jobs that require college degrees. The Pew Economic Mobility Projects (2013) reports that 10 percent of recent university graduates are unemployed and 26 percent are under-employed in high-school level jobs. I didn't provide these statistics to make you depressed; I provided them to apprise you that the book you are now holding will help you scale the interview hurdle and become a part of the work force.

Secondly, you are a *superior* product. Superior means preeminent, top of the line, premium, achieving the highest seal, built to last. You received a quality education and were taught by quality professors. What you gained throughout your scholastic career should now be put on display; your skills should portray how you have been sharpened and prepared for a lasting career. Following the guidelines in this book will cause *you* to be in demand. Ask any business owner who creates quality products, what are the five key things to building a quality brand? Building Quality (Beckerman 2013) is made up of these five things:

1. Continuous improvement philosophy
2. Consistency in everything you do
3. Teamwork as part of the culture
4. Routine measure and analysis
5. Training for all

These five key aspects are indicative of what makes *you* so important and why you are needed in corporate America.

1. **Continuous improvement philosophy.** Everything and anything can be improved. You should seek to continuously improve your skills and level of influence in your career field. Service learning is an excellent way to build and develop those fundamentals skills that will be salient to your future.
2. **Consistency in everything you do.** You must strive for consistency in every area of your life. You will have a certain degree of standardization but it should not inhibit creativity. Have you ever met someone who behaves inconsistently? You will find this person can't be counted on.

Can your boss, manager, or supervisor count on you? Does your word mean anything?

3. **Teamwork as part of the culture.** Teamwork by definition means the process of working collaboratively with a group of people in order to achieve a goal. You must have heard the adage, "teamwork makes the dream work." Believe me, it does. I know many students dislike the thought of working within a group. However, teamwork is unavoidable in corporate America.

Since you are a part of a team then it's important who you network and connect yourself with organizations that will help sharpen your skills. Service learning through college and universities, utilizing LinkedIn, American Express and other legit business forums gives hands-on information and puts you in the know of current business skills both internally and outside the organization.

4. **Routine measure and analysis.** It's important to always assess your performance at work and on a project. Why? It helps one become consistent and deliver excellence. Bekerman (2013) states you can use measurement to deliver more consistent products and services. This will even help you address and solve occurring problems to reduce potential damage or costly expenses.

5. **Training.** Staying current with your certifications is recommended. Staying current is also important because it sharpens your skill level. Training workshops and education are significant building blocks within an organization to make all other elements work. Self-assured employees (such as you) need to understand what goals need to be accomplished. Knowing the changes that are about to take place and how this may affect the company or even you position is vital. Participating in workshops or professional development programs the company offers, or maybe just volunteering to spearhead a project, can serve as a launching pad for something more. For example, you may take enough professional development workshops to the point where you are able to develop your own training program and companies will pay you to facilitate them – it's just a thought.

80 Interview Questions & Answers:

Questions and Answers about self

1. **Tell me a little about yourself.**
   It's not easy to sum up your life in a few sentences. A great way to answer this question is to develop a 60-second biographical sketch that emphasizes your pattern of interests, skills and accomplishments. *(gowrikumar.com)*
   - State your key accomplishments at school or at previous jobs.
   - State the strengths you developed as a result of those accomplishments.
   - State how these relate to the job for which you're applying.
   - This is a good time to sell your service learning experience (for college students) or employment accomplishments. Hint: Help the interviewer by focusing your reply on this question: *What about you would be most relevant to their company's needs?*

Here is an answer tip:

- I have been in the field for _____ years and have worked for _____ years as a (*State Job position and title*) at (*Company name*).
  Currently I am a (*State Job position and title*) at (*Company Name*).
  I received my degree in _(*state major*)_ (w) honors and while attending *(name the college or university)*.
  I was selected and/or worked for _____. I provided service learning (only if applies to you) at/or obtained an internship at _____. I enjoy the challenge of my work/internship, and find I have major strengths to offer for this position.
  I have _____ (*list your strengths, briefly*).
    o   Analytical proficiency which is great for _____
    o   Acute attention to detail critical for _____
    o   Fact finding ability which allows me to _____
  Express affiliations/certifications, For ex., NAN (National Association of Nurses)

2. **How would you describe yourself?**

   Think about action words and connect them to the position you are applying for. Try to tie in your responsibilities with those listed in the job description for the new position. This will help the employer see that you have the qualifications necessary to do the job.

Here are some answer tips:

- I would describe myself as a detailed-oriented, critical thinker who is able to execute my responsibilities proficiently. As a ____ (*fill in job title for which you are applying*), it is extremely important that I thoroughly cover all information with my clients in order to secure the contract. I will need to think quickly and to adapt to any situation. Omitting pertinent information can result in a loss of money and time. For instance, I recall when I worked for _____ there was an oversight in the booking department and _____ (*Be specific about what you did and the outcome*).

- I am a passionate self-directed, strong communicator who utilizes my time management skills efficiently. I believe in the 80/20 rule when needed – that's 80 percent of the work in 20 percent of the time. As a ____ (*state your major or current interest*), I sometimes have to __ (*share something concrete about what you do*; then connect it to their ideal candidate, which happens to be you).

3. **How would your manager describe you?**

Here is an answer tip:

- My managers would describe me in one word: driven. I am someone who would rather work tirelessly to overcome obstacles on my own as opposed to continuously seeking managerial guidance. I try to make my managers' lives easier in this way. For example, when I first started working at __ (*name of organization*), I was asked to figure out ways to cut costs. Instead of relying on my manager, who has other projects to oversee, I decided to learn about __ (*provide key issue*) so I could better understand it.

- For example, transportation logistics is behind the transporting of millions of iPhones from China to the U.S. my employer needed for each facility. I decided to take a look at the overhead cost factor and scale down shipping costs dramatically. My efforts saved us 30 percent, which equated to about $50,000 after our first quarterly shipping. After seeing what worked best and what could be improved, I took this information to my manager who was grateful for my initiative; he then implemented my key suggestions (Satariano, 2013).

- The key is to be specific with something you did no matter how large or small, and provide the outcome. When you mention numbers, it is always a plus.

4. **What's one quality you dislike about yourself?**
   This question is obviously not about beauty or looks but more about your characteristics. Link your response to areas that connect to the job.

Answer tips:

- I sometimes overthink situations, looking for every possible error or mistake that needs to be addressed. But, I try not to spend too much time on unnecessary areas pertaining to (*name the issue*); this doesn't help me excel in my job.
- I get impatient with individuals who don't put forth the effort they should. Follow-up with a quick example and how you have adjusted.
  - o For example, I worked at Target for three years as a security representative. I was one of the first to notify my supervisor of fraudulent activities. Fraud is a major issue here in the U.S. Unfortunately, my warning wasn't taken seriously so I decided to take action and go above my manager [something I would never do unless…] and the result of our security breach was devastating. Personal data was stolen from more than 61 million customers (Seals, 2014). This cost us millions. The end result was the following…my department had to:
    - Appoint a chief information security officer
    - Keep a written information security program, which will document potential security risks, and develop metrics to measure the security of its systems
    - Offer security training to "relevant" workers, educating them about the importance of safeguarding personal identifying information (Target Fraud Prevention Department, 2015).

QUESTIONS AND ANSWERS ABOUT THE INDUSTRY

5. **Why do you want to work in this industry?**

Tell a story about how you first became interested in this type of work. Point out any similarities between the job you're interviewing for, and your current and most recent job. Provide proof that you aren't simply shopping in this interview. Make your passion for your work a theme that you allude to continually throughout the interview.

Here is an answer tip:

*   I've always wanted to work in an industry that makes tools. One of my hobbies is home-improvement projects, so I've collected a number of saws manufactured by your company. I could be an accountant anywhere, but I'd rather work for a company whose products I trust.

Here is an answer tip for Education majors:

*   I've always wanted to work with children. I can recall using my dolls as my students and creating a classroom atmosphere even as a child. My passion for the field started when I did my internship at __ (*organization name*). This was an amazing experience. I was extremely impressed with how I was able to help 3rd graders develop a fondness for science and math. In addition, while working at __ (*organization name*) the students' test scores improved by 78 percent and FCAT proficiency by 45 percent. Some even majored in math and science, which is highly beneficial to the STEM track.
*   *Word to the wise*: the FCAT is no longer being used. It has been replaced with the End of Course Exam (EOC). So make sure your response reflects knowledge of current examinations.

Here is an answer tip for Pharmaceutical majors:

*   I enjoyed my statistics, math and science courses the most while attending __ (*name of institution*). When I was able to intern in the pharmaceutical department at __ (*organization name*), my passion for this industry continued. I was able to shadow the clinical pharmacist during rounds and observed how (he or she – pick one) provided pharmacotherapy interventions to improve health outcomes. I am now applying to your

organization and looking forward to continued research in genomics. I have a strong background in science and I believe the future of medicine will be understanding man's genetic code and developing drugs to combat certain diseases. I have also noticed that strokes are soaring among the geriatric population and in the biotechnology field I can make a difference. I want to be a part of a company that's leading the way.

Here is an answer tip for Healthcare majors:

- I've always had a love for the health care industry, but my interest in working in health care really started when I volunteered at a neighborhood clinic. I knew our department capabilities were amazing but the staff needed to practice better patient care services. So I worked with management to come up with a strategy that increased our patient satisfaction rates by 55 percent in a year. I have a background in business management, so I thought I could use this to my advantage. We created an Introduction of Management Systems workshop for all personnel. The emphasis of the training was on quality care and cost recovery. Our experience showed that putting a system in place to attract patients who can afford to pay for high quality services and enjoy quality care treatment would then allow us to use this same system to be extended to non-paying patients. It was great to be able to contribute positively to an industry I feel so passionately about, and to help promote a clinic I really believed in (AllHealthcare, 2016).

6. **How do you stay current in your industry?**

   Demonstrate natural interest in the industry or career field by describing publications or trade associations that are compatible with your goal.

Here is an answer tip:

- I pore over the *Wall Street Journal, Washington Post*, the *Miami Herald*, the *New York Times, Institutional Investor*, and several mutual fund newsletters. I have a number of friends who are analysts (or whatever the career field may be). I also try to stay connected with LinkedIn.

7.   **What is our distinctive advantage within the industry?**

Describe things you believe this company does very well, particularly compared to its competition. Explain how the financial strength of the company is important.

Here are some answer tips:

- With your low-cost-producer status and headquarters operation in a low-cost area of the country, you seem to be in a better position to be able to spend aggressively on research and development (R&D), even in a down year, compared to your closest rival.
- This hospital's most distinctive advantage within this industry is customer care. In a perfect world, a company's day-to-day operations are managed for peak performance, so that it maximizes its profits while minimizing its risks, costs and losses. Your organization has been able to minimize those risks factors by... (*Mention something they were able to do*). For example, if you work in a medical facility you may say, "Our department provided services within the administrative policy to create the most efficient process for quick, yet appropriate discharge. This discharge was essential to the appropriate post-acute setting and follow-ups with our patients."

8.   **Why do you think this industry would sustain your interest over the long haul?**
What expectations or projects do you have for your career field? What truly excites you? What proof can you offer that your interest has already come from a deep curiosity – perhaps going back at least a few years – rather than a current whim you'll outgrow? I decided to take a more scientific approach to this question.

Here is an answer tip for Biology majors:

- I received my first taste of the scientific process as an undergraduate at __ (*name of institution*). As a biology major, I took courses with dynamic professors that provided a solid foundation in classical ecology and evolutionary theory, but it was my independent research experience that inspired me to go into science. My research focused on the influence of invasive species in meadow plant community. As my research questions evolved, I became increasingly interested in the role of plant-microbial interactions in community ecology and ecosystem function. As I continue my research and studies I look forward to the unknown and to greater discoveries.

Here is an answer tip for Senior Chemistry & Forensic Science majors:

- I was always captivated by the crime television shows such as *Cold Cases*, *Criminal Minds* and *FBI's Unsolved Mysteries*. These shows solved crimes using cutting edge laboratory techniques to link suspects to crime scenes. Never having been exposed to the concept of DNA, I found it amazing that suspects could be identified by blood, saliva or even a single strand of hair. I found myself completely entranced by the idea that I could be the one conducting molecular experiments in a lab, making discoveries. Several years later I had a chance to fulfill this desire. My first research experience was in Philadelphia at the Monell Chemical Senses Center (*or wherever you actually had a research experience*) where I began as a summer apprentice. While there, I developed whole genome microarray technology for the identification of phylogenetically conserved DNA sequence. Because of the fundamental importance of genes to all biology, I decided to apply to PhD programs in order to continue basic genetic studies with the hope of eventually conducting translation genetic research. I can't stop now! (Boston University Arts & Science Program, 2016)

Here is an answer tip for Nursing students:

- I've always loved nursing, but my interest in health care really started when I volunteered at a homeless shelter in college. Seeing so many people without care inspired me to pursue a career devoted to caring for others. I kept going back and volunteering, which got me hooked. It was great to be able to contribute positively to society that then led me to a field I feel so passionate about (Nursinglink.com, 2016).

QUESTIONS AND ANSWERS ABOUT THE COMPANY

9. **Why our company/organization?**

Suggestion tip: Describe your first encounter or a recent encounter with the company or its products and services. What would be particularly motivating to you about working there… as opposed to a different company? The recruiter will look for evidence of genuine interest and more than just surface research on the company.

Here is an answer tip for Journalism majors:

- I served as an intern at the *Miami Herald* for three years and I followed all the corporate blogs and social networking sites, and I notice your organization has opened an avenue for small businesses to get visibility *(now connect this to their mission statement)*... you are doing this on a global scale.

Here is an answer tip for Journalism Field:

- I served as an intern at the *Miami Herald* for three years and I followed all the corporate blogs and social networking sites, and I notice your organization has opened an avenue for small businesses to get visibility *(now connect this to their mission statement)*... you are doing this on a global scale. For example, _____ motto *(be specific about the organization name and slogan)* (for instance) "where energy and synergy comes together" speaks for itself. This organization has been instrumental in climate change and the ever-increasing energy demand in our society. You also play an active role in reducing your carbon footprint and building more energy-efficient campuses/facilities. Conserving the energy and water used on campus is paramount for sustainability. As a writer, I pay special attention to matters such as these and I like to write about organizations that are environmentally friendly. I worked at ABC University for two years and I fulfilled a variety of duties which included reporting, news/feature writing, researching, and fact-checking pertinent information. I hope to continue this at your organization.

  Another suggestion tip: Mention the company's slogan, goals, vision or maybe a portion of their mission statement. Elaborate on it, connect it to real life issues or back to yourself and/or your work ethic. This will immediately add to the interviewer's interest in you.

Here is an answer tip - Community Health/Community Service:

- I chose to apply for this position because I have devoted my time to working with patients directly to improve health status in the community. While I was looking for an agency to enhance my skills, I noticed that your company is one that offers me this opportunity.
- Your slogan says "opening the door to brighter health." According to ___ (specify where you got your source) currently there are over 20 million adults who are uninsured in the United States and 61 percent *(make sure*

if you use statistics they are accurate. Why? Because if this information is incorrect you will blow the interview) of them said the primary reason they are uninsured is because the cost of insurance is too high or they have lost their job (U.S. Census). Your slogan suggests that you genuinely care about helping people improve their health, and won't turn away a patient in need.

- Another reason I chose your organization is because of your contributions to the community. For example, under the direction of (*name of individual*), associate professor and program coordinator for the Interior Design program, students painted a home and decorated it with items found almost exclusively from the Habitat ReStore. The Habitat ReStore accepts donations of new and gently used building materials, appliances, furniture, cabinets, tools and other home improvement items and then sells them to the public at a fraction of the retail price.

- Finally, your partnership with Miami Dade College highlights the ability of the ReStore to keep usable materials out of the waste stream and provide affordable options for buying home building, remodeling and creative arts supplies. All ReStore proceeds benefit Habitat for Humanity's local affordable housing program and the underprivileged who desperately needs these services. I want to be a part of a company that is innovative and exhibits foster care.

Here is an answer tip for Physician Assistant majors:

- It all started during a chemistry class back in my freshman year when I was asked, "If I had the energy to create a magical power, what would it be?" I replied, "To eradicate every disease known to mankind." I had big dreams then and I still do today. I was able to intern at the CDC Undergraduate Public Health Scholars (CUPS) program for six months, and followed all the disaster preparedness and first aid stations (2016).

- Throughout my internship I participated in leadership training and an orientation to the public health disciplines, and gained real world work experiences through quality patient care (*Be specific about what you did*). If given the opportunity to become part of your team, I can ensure that every patient will leave our office with a sense of security and reassurance that their medical issues are in good hands.

- During my research, I also noticed that your organization consistently receives the highest patient satisfaction ratings such at the *5 Star Awards for Overall Quality Care* and the *LEED for Healthcare Designation* which is really impressive. I can see how providing the highest quality patient care is not "just talk," but a reality for ____ (name the company). I want to be a part of a company that is breaking barriers and setting industry standards.

10. **What have you learned about our company from customers, employees, or others?**

    Describe how your interest has grown from personal dealings with the company representatives. Think creatively in preparing for job interviews. For example, prior to your job interview, speak with retailers or workers at other distribution points about the company's product line. What can they tell you? Give one or two examples why you're interested in this company. What's the most compelling example you can describe to prove your interest?

Here is an answer tip:

• I actually called several of the key customers mentioned in your brochure. Two of the customers I spoke with explained why they continued to buy from you year after year. Your distribution operation is phenomenal. Are there any service improvements you are still planning to make?

11. **From your resume, I notice that you interned at a small investment banking boutique. Did you pursue a full-time job offer with them? What happened?**

    Describe a specific issue that took place and what was the outcome. Then shared your approach to the situation and the choice you had to make.

Here is an answer tip:

• Yes, I did very well at my internship, and I had originally assumed that I would come on staff once I graduated from college. However, _____ (name of company) drastically cut back the number of new hires they were planning. As fate would have it, they will not be hiring any of the interns they had last summer. I love working at _____ (name of company), and I brought some references with me today to show you that my job performance there was stellar. Still, in some ways, I consider this new turn of events to be a lucky break for me, believe it or not.

12. **Tell me what you know about this company.**

    Describe your first encounter or a recent encounter with the company or its products and services. What would be particularly motivating to you about working there as opposed to working the same type of job in a different company? The recruiter will look for evidence of genuine interest and more than just surface research on the company. Reciting the annual report isn't likely to impress most recruiters, but feedback and reviews from customers and employees will.

Here is an answer tip for Hospitality Management majors:

- I served as an intern to a restaurant analyst last summer and followed all the steak-house chains closely. I noticed what __ *(name the company)* has done especially well is focus on a limited menu with great consistency among locations; the business traveler trusts your product anywhere in the U.S. I'm particularly interested in learning from experts such as yourselves, while at the same time helping to set targets to increase your revenues. Whether it is through food and beverage retail services, or simply your room accommodation services, I look forward to being part of a winning team. As business writer Michelle Reynold's (2015) once said, "…how accomplished you and your staff are at serving others will determine your business' level of success" (p. 3).

Here is an answer tip for Culinary Arts majors/Community Service:

- I recently graduated from the (include the school name)__ School of Culinary Arts. I came across your ad through a video blog. I was quite surprised because your company's humanitarian focus is on the Incentives for Cultural Shifts Campaign. I grew up in a signal parent household, with six siblings. It was difficult for my mother to provide for us, but thanks to these [incentive] meals, we were able to survive. I joined The Food Recovery Network project (2016) at __ *(school name)*; it started off as a group of students who collected leftovers from our dining center and donated them to the homeless. Then, I started working for the ___ *(organization)*, providing free service to the community. I get pure joy knowing that what I do is making a difference, even in a small way. I am hoping you will give me an opportunity to do the same and even more.

13. **How will you complement this department?**

    Suggestion Tip: Describe how your personality and/or skills would help round out the department. What types of people enjoy working with you for hours at a time? How would the company's customers or clients react? Assure the interviewer that there will be no surprises about your work personality.

Here is an answer tip for Computer Animation majors:

• I enjoy an environment in which people bounce ideas off each other and have the flexibility to ask for help when they need it. I'm usually a great troubleshooter for PC problems in my office, and I often ask for help to proofread important memos. I believe in give-and-take. I also enjoy bouncing ideas back and forth with my co-workers to see what needs improving as a computer animator. Writing codes that determine how accurate and lifelike animated scenes and characters will be can be a challenge. But I am up for the task, especially with this great staff I look forward to working with.

14. **What is a major challenge this company/career field faces?**
Obviously, if you haven't been reading about changes and advancement the company has...you will get stuck. Don't ever put yourself at a standstill!

Here is an answer tip for a Structural Engineer:

• In an increasingly interconnected, volatile and uncertain world, it's clear that the risk landscape is changing. Both the speed at which risk events occur and the extent to which they have spread has risen dramatically. While navigating through turbulent times, your company has shown a lot of "resilience." I think one of the most challenging aspects that I have had to navigate through in this career field is determining the structural integrity of a building. Making sure building projects are able to withstand all types of stress is critical in this field.

Here is an answer tip for an entry-level Nuclear Physicist:

• Well in this line of work, the word "anticipation" is the key to everything. Anticipating problems before they arise and implementing safety procedures is paramount in this line of work. During my tenure with the Nuclear Mechanical Apprentice Program (NMAP, 2015), I did routine decontamination work. I oversaw the monitoring of equipment and their effluent paths. Monitored radiation releases and took proper precautions to contain the gases. I also provided samples of liquids, gases and solids which had to be analyzed, and recorded. Lastly, I did routine radiation and contamination surveys along with heat stress sampling. -https://jobs.entergy.com/

15. **What's your dream job?**

    This is your ideal chance to sell your aptitudes that fit the job description. Showing an interest in finding new ways these skills can be put to use in a new job with additional responsibilities. Tie in the industry, size of company, etc.

Here is an answer tip for entry-level International Relations majors:

• My dream job would include many of the responsibilities and duties required for this position. Your plans call for expanding internationally during the next year is very exciting for me especially because I am trilingual and would be able to work in your South American or Asian branches. I know this kind of work requires a deep understanding of the cultures, customs, morals and even religious views that predominate in various countries. As a paid intern for Uline International Shipping Supply Services *(wherever you work)*, I enjoyed providing weekly analysis of international customers' feedback, assisting International Operations management with monthly reports, and creating competitor analysis on various topics (Monster.com).

QUESTIONS AND ANSWERS ABOUT YOUR ACADEMIC TRAINING

This is your ideal chance to combine theory with practicum. Don't stay stuck in the classroom; share how you have been able to use the knowledge gained in the classroom through work, internship or service learning.

16. **How has your academic training prepared you for this position/ career field?**

Here is an answer tip for Nursing majors:

• Recently received _____ degree in _____ from _____. I took courses in Introduction to Nursing, Human Anatomy & Physiology & Microbiology. My classes, together with my clinical experiences, have prepared me well to begin working at __ *(name the company or healthcare organization)*. My classes exposed me to the most up-to-date research in our field, and through my clinical rotation, I gained a lot of insight and confidence in working with patients under my supervisor's direction.

Here is an answer tip for Funeral Science majors:

• I recently received a _____ degree from _____ in_____ w/honors. While at the university, my studies included Embalming 1 & 2, Restorative Arts 1 & 2, Funeral Directing, and Funeral Home Operations, etc. While attending the university, I was able to work full-time at Boyd's Funeral Home and especially learned how to console and comfort grieving family members during their difficult time. Communicated with the city council to issue death certificates; and coordinated with newspapers agencies to issue obituaries. I am also affiliated with Cremation Association of Florida & National Funeral Directors (Monster.com).

Here is an answer tip for Healthcare majors:

• After earning my Bachelors in Health Science from Nova Southeastern University, I held an internship position at the Harding Oncology Center in Miami, Florida. This gave me hands-on experience with cancer patients, and now I am anxious to use my knowledge to specialize in cancer treatment. In addition, my clinical training in the ER of Aventura Hospital prepared me for the fast-paced care required of an ER Physician Assistant.

• I also had the opportunity to work as a research assistant for Dr. Ray at Aventura Hospital who was writing about new findings in the treatment of heart disease. The knowledge I gained during that time prepared me for assisting with cardiac patients in a more effective way. I have always envisioned myself working as part of a team. The PA path resonated with me as teamwork is a fundamental facet of this career field.

Here is answer tip for Biology majors:

• I received my first taste of the scientific process as a graduate at Harvard School of Medicine. I took courses in General Biology I & II, and General & Organic Chemistry I & II. This provided a solid foundation in classical ecology and evolutionary theory. My independent research in the influence of invasive species in the meadow plant community (*mention a particular research*) was my inspiration. As my research questions evolved, I became increasingly interested in the role of plant-microbial interactions in community ecology and ecosystem function. I discovered that invasive microbes, plants and animals are a major threat to the composition and functioning of ecosystems; however, the mechanistic basis of why exotic species can be so abundant and disruptive is not well understood. As I continued my research and studies I look forward to the unknown and greater discoveries. (ISME, Journal 2016)

17. **Which course was particularly challenging?**
The interviewer will want to see how well you respond to difficult situations. Demonstrate that you won't fold in the face of difficulty, and that you're willing to put in the extra effort to meet a challenge.

Here is an answer tip for Chemistry majors:

- Initially, I was completely overwhelmed by the introductory chemistry course that I took last year. No matter how hard I studied, I seemed to be getting nowhere. So I tried a new approach. Instead of just studying by myself, I asked a friend Sally a chemistry major to study with me. I also began to seek help from the professor after class. I found that the more time I spent in the lab was beneficial. I ended up with a B+ in the course and thought I achieved a solid understanding of the material. More than that, I learned that tackling a new field of study sometimes requires a new approach, not just hard work, and that the help of others can be crucial!

18. **Why didn't you participate more in extracurricular activities?**
The interviewer may be worried that if you don't have many outside interests, you may eventually suffer from burnout. Employers like candidates who are well rounded. If you didn't participate in formal extracurricular activities in college, you still may want to talk about some of your interests, such as reading or exercising, or that you may have a passion for running even if you weren't on the college track team.

Here is an answer tip STEM Majors:

- I wanted to give as much effort as possible to my studies. I came from a high school in a very small town. I received A's but that still did not prepare me well for college. I studied harder, I found time to explore and give back to my local community. During my studies at __ (list the institution) New York City College of Technology I participated in the Solar Decathlon. Our team took an urban approach to a resilient, energy-efficient housing that adapted to the needs of a diverse city and its population. We call our project "DURA"-Diverse, Urban, Resilient, and Adaptable. Because superstorm Sandy devastated communities throughout New York City, our DURA project was resilient to respond to such disasters. The project had four main aspects:

- The use of the 5.9-kW PV array of 19 panels generated electricity, while solar thermal panels provided hot water.
- The use of a low-entropy recovery ventilator regulated indoor temperature and humidity and supplied constant fresh air.
- The use of rainwater from the roof was harvested and stored in tanks for watering the outdoor garden and green wall.
- The use of the home automation system monitored temperature, humidity, light levels, and motion throughout the house and helped balance energy used

This challenge has developed my analytical, critical thinking and communication skills. We wound up taking 2nd place in the overall competition. (Taken from U.S. Department of Energy-Solar Competitions, 2016)

QUESTIONS AND ANSWERS ABOUT CAREER GOALS

19. **What are your Career Goals?**
Hint: Refer to your objective statement on your resume and then give a specific task you will work to execute. Developing **SMART** (*s*pecific, *m*easurable, *a*chievable, *r*esults that are *t*ime driven) goals that will enhance. Be brief and to the point; include short-term and long-term objectives.

Here is a suggestion/answer tip:

- I have learned that long-term goals are best achieved when broken into shorter goals. My short-term career goal is hopefully to join your organization and contribute as much as I can to its success. As for my long-term career goal, it's to grow with your company, and continue to add value at even higher levels.

Here is an answer tip Law Enforcement majors:

- I know the goal of any police officer is to stop crime and enforce laws. We all accomplish it together by Patrol, Investigation and Community Relations. I currently work for City of Miami Police Department (*or wherever you decide)* and one major challenge the city battles is gun violence. The department implemented the Smart Policing Initiative Gun Violence Spotlight Program. Our goal was to target persistent gun violence "hot spots" and whether it was through prevention, intervention or suppression we saw a significant decrease in violent crimes. The department implemented a simple system called the Chronic Offender Bulletin. The bulletin contained pertinent information about each offender which was then distributed statewide. Each offender was placed into an online folder based on the location of their stop. These bulletins were updated every three months and every officer had access through our patrol car computers. This initiative was a major success and exceeded the department's goals. (Smart Policing.com)

Here is an answer tip for "long term" goal Physician Assistant majors:

- My long-term goal will be to affiliate with professionals like you to work together to develop a comprehensive tobacco prevention program. I believe in supporting strategic efforts to protect the public's health from the harmful effects of tobacco use. As part of a team, I want to add value and continue to grow the company by providing strategic leadership, a solid scientific base, and technical assistance to advance evidence-based interventions worldwide.

Here is an answer tip for Physical Therapy majors:

- One of my goals is to work with injured soldiers who use prosthetics to help these individuals reclaim independence and increase their mobility. Tailoring exercise programs that provide the most benefit with the least amount of discomfort is essential. I also look forward to assisting with their gait training, progressive strengthening, teaching my patient proper balance and appropriate prosthetic management all of which will help in the recovery process.

Here is an answer tip Psychiatrist Majors:

- One of my goals is to use CBT (Cognitive Behavior Therapy) to treat schizophrenic patients to improve their quality of life. This is a chronic disorder so the goal wouldn't be to "cure" it, but rather improve my patient's ability to become functionally independent and to reduce the distress they experience in their daily lives.

Here is an answer tip for Mass Communication majors:

- I developed an interest in TV production while taking courses in entertainment and technology. To challenge that interest I started my own...while attending Barry University. I also applied for service learning through a TV internship at Channel 4/Neighbors 4 (*tell them what you gained as a result of the internship*). Now I am looking for a promising entry level position as a production assistant at this company.

20. **Describe a major goal you've set for yourself recently.**
    Give an example of a goal you set and achieved. Ideally, this should be a professional goal such as improving time management skills, achieving new performance targets, or learning a new skill. A personal example can also be appropriate if it reinforces your pattern of accomplishments.

Here is a suggestion tip:

- For example, if you take a great deal of initiative and quickly move into leadership positions, you might use a personal example relating to your recent community work: I organized a community walk-a-thon that raised $30,000 in matching funds to purchase new computers for the local library.
- Talk about your results. This indicates you set realistic goals and that you can focus on outcomes. Select an example that has interesting outcomes related to your efforts. The example should showcase your skills and abilities.

Here is an answer tip for Biology majors:

- A major goal I have had is to try to uncover the mechanism of signaling translocation in the compound eye of the fruit fly. While trying to discover how these tiny little insects [have eyes that contain 100 hundreds of lights sensing unit] were able to move protein responsible for producing what they consider vision, I decided to pursue a PhD at _ (*name the institution*). Fast forward to today, surprisingly I still work on the fruit fly project.

21. **Where do you see yourself five years from now?**
    This open-ended question is one of the most difficult and stressful ones job seekers face. Employers supposedly ask this question because they are looking for people who know what they want to do and are focused on specific professional goals. If you lack goals, you will have difficulty answering this question.

Be sure you arrive at the interview with a clear vision of what you want to do today, tomorrow and five years from now. Be consistent with the objective on your resume and the skills and accomplishments you're communicating to the interviewer. Your answer should be employer-centered. Do not indicate that you hope to start your own business. Such responses indicate a lack of long-term interest since you do not plan to be around for long.

Here is an answer tip Law Enforcement majors:

- In five years, I see myself within this organization working with your terrorism and surveillance team. I look forward to identifying and implementing approaches for addressing crime and fear that can more effectively reduce both reported and non-reported crimes of all types. The changes made in communication between local and national intelligence units since the September 11 attacks can be put into three categories: culture, capability, and awareness according to the Police Chief Magazine. I look forward to working with this team (Downing, 2016).

Here is another answer tip:

- Ideally, I would like to work for a company such as this one and within five years, become a project specialist in the Outreach Department. In five years, I hope to be working towards two objectives: increasing sustainable practices and reducing outsourced spending.

Here is an answer tip for IT Majors:

- My aim over the next five years is to develop my knowledge and skills in the latest software programs, and become even more proficient in today's programs, such as JAVA, Oracle and C++. In addition, I am interested in better understanding the clients' needs, researching current market trends, and becoming a full-fledged software developer.

22. **What are your Strengths and Weaknesses?**
   Remember it is a **two part** question. Elaborate on your strengths first. This is a great example of what is known as a negative question. Negative questions are a favorite among interviewers, because they're effective for uncovering problems or weaknesses. The key to answering negative questions is to give them a positive spin.

Answer/Suggestion tip:

- My strengths are two-fold, strong ____ & ___. Then make a brief statement about one or both that's relevant to the job position. Suggestion tip: Mention a skill that was once a weakness and discuss/demonstrate how it is now your strength. Always provide concrete examples of what you're doing to:
  - *Fix* the problem.
  - *State Progress* that you've made.
  - *Improvements* to help the department or the employer.

Here is an answer tip for Civil Engineer majors:

- My strengths are two-fold; strong drafting skills & certification in CADD software. As a junior civil engineer, I helped design streets and drainage systems, and participated in materials testing and construction inspections. I also ___ (*quickly explain the two strengths by providing concrete examples and then link it back to the position you are applying for*) (Monster.com)..

Here is another answer tip:

- My strengths are my interpersonal skills, and usually I can persuade people easily. I have good judgment about people and an intuitive sense of their talents and ability to contribute to a given problem. These skills seem to be directly related to the job. Though three years' work experience is required for this job, my resume shows I've only have __(#)__ years' experience. However, it doesn't show that I took two evening college courses to enhance my skills and that I am an active member of the ____ society. I also try to gain knowledge by reading the industry's trade journals. I'm certain that my combined knowledge and skill level are the equivalent to that of other people who may have three years' or more of work experience. By-the-way, I'm also currently enrolled in a time-management course, and can already see the effects of this course at work on my present job.

23. **What is your greatest weakness?**
    First, when you respond, remember to never say the word "weakness;" mention "challenge" or "area to be improved" instead. For this particular question your best bet is to admit to a weakness that isn't catastrophic, inconsistent, or currently disruptive to your chosen professional field, and to emphasize how you've overcome or minimized the problem.

Here is an answer tip:

- I admit to being a bit of a perfectionist. I take a great deal of pride in my work and am committed to producing the highest-quality work I can. Sometimes if I'm not careful, I can go a bit overboard. I've learned that it's not always possible or even practical to try to perfect one work; sometimes you have to decide what's important and ignore the rest in order to be productive. It's a question of trade-offs. I now pay a lot of attention to pacing my work, so that I don't get too caught up in perfecting every last detail.

Here is an answer tip:

- My greatest issue is my intolerance to laziness and lack of team work because when a team member withholds important information to the detriment of his or her peers or the assignment's success, this can be quite upsetting. I have always tried to maximize knowledge-sharing by bring team members together prior to launching any assignment to ensure everyone is on the same page. Yet, there are times when team members don't comply. In those instances, I have learned to speak privately with the individual(s) to understand just why pertinent information was withheld from the group.

Here is an answer tip:

- I often hold others to the same professional expectations I hold for myself. This leads to great disappointment when people fail to perform up to expectations. I have learned to use this as an opportunity to inspire, rather than criticize, my teammates to take greater ownership of their work and perform as expected.

Suggestion Tip: Use words like "challenge, issue, current problem, concern" instead of "weakness." Mention one or two statements below and then give an example of how you overcame it.

The following lists are random areas of concerns in the workplace

• Lack of funding	• Building code zone
• Unethical practices	• Rude customers
• Unproductive working environment	• Corrupt politicians
• Micromanagement	• Raising admission standards
• When leads go cold…	• Stagnation in the industry
• Unsolved murders, cases	• Lack of qualified _____
• Youth aging out of the system	• Gaps between race, culture, age,
• Lack of parental involvement	• Limited resources for special needs population etc…
• Overcrowding in ____	• Violence in the local community
• Increasing influence of off-shore…	• Quality service
• Gender bias	

24. **Why are you leaving your current job?**
    Suggestion tip: Focus on why you want to **move** to the target company. "I am eager to take on more challenges" (**Be specific** about what you mean here).

Here is an answer tip:

• The company I am currently working for is merging with another establishment and as a result, my department will be made redundant. You can also mention any of the following:

   • **Seasonal position or grant-funded**....
   • **Outsourcing**
   • **Downsizing**
   • **Relocation (military, medical reasons)**
   • **Fired/Incarcerated**
   • **Kat's: CLAMPS Formula** (Challenge, Location, Advancement, Management, Prestige, Security). Mention these and connect it to the current position you are seeking. Be specific with a brief example.

Here is an answer tip for recent college Veterinary Graduates

• I am leaving my current job due to management cut backs. With the recent layoffs and reduced work hours I am looking for a better option. While working for ___ (name of company) I assisted in the response and recovery for endangered animals. I enjoyed the collaborative nature of this line of work and my passion for animals is endless. I know this company has worked hard to help exotic animals receive quality care and be restored to their natural habitat. I want to continue in this career path and working with this organization will provide this opportunity.

Here is an answer tip for entry level lawyers:

• I recently graduated from Harvard School of Law. During my tenure there I interned at the Harvard Kennedy School, where I achieved the following:
   • I wrote opinion pieces on presidential powers and questions regarding executive authority.
   • I researched and drafted portions of civil rights legislation considered by Congress.

- I drafted position papers on separation of the church, state and charitable choice issues.

The knowledge and skills I gained through this experience are essential for the position I am applying for today. I have decided it's time for me to move forward to sharpen and broaden my knowledge in this field and use the critical skills gained by applying at your firm.

Here is an answer for a person that was incarcerated:

- Unfortunately, I made some poor decisions during my teens. Those poor choices, coupled with a harsh living environment, led me down the wrong path and caused me to make the wrong type of friends. I got myself into some unexplainable situations and lost my job [*tread lightly here, it's not what you say but how and the way you respond*]. I was in the wrong place at the wrong time and lost __ years of my life.

- However, while I was detained, I took the opportunity to reassess and make some strategic changes in my life. I finished my high school GED. I also gained hands-on experience working for the Vermont Department of Corrections Work Release Program (2015). The program provided me with critical skills in (_____). The program helped refine my social and living skills, taught me how to manage my personal finances, and gave me hands-on experience in (_____) all while under supervision. The knowledge and skills I gained are essential for the position I am applying for today (Monster.com).

25. **What are some challenges in this industry?**
    The employer wants to know what are some major challenges in your career field and how do you stay on top of your game. So be specific with how you handle a key challenge.

Here is an answer tip for Accounting Majors:

- Well, in this field one of the biggest challenges we encounter is keeping up with new accounting standards. I am a fast learner and realize that constantly updating my skills is important in order to compete. When I got hired to work in this industry my first task was to stay current with these changes. I did so through the Financial Accounting Standard Board (FASB) website I checked this frequently for changes. I also search the IRS website for tax law changes. Bad accounting practices and failure to stay current represent the potential for significant business loss one in which no can afford. I'd say staying up to date has given me the competitive edge. (DiGiovanni, 2015)

Here is an answer tip for Oceanography majors:

- In this field, overfishing and climate change have been major issues. To overcome these challenges, I started an anti-whaling campaign at _____ and am a spokesperson for the Greenpeace organization. My goal in these endeavors is to bring greater awareness to these pervasive issues.

Here is an answer tip for Environmental Science majors:

- A major impact concerning the oceans today is climate change. Carbon emissions from cars and industries keep the heat from the sun close to the surface of the earth, which then warms the ocean. I started a petition that snowballed into a bill to help reduce our role in contributing to carbon emissions. This bill has led to stronger sustainability projects. I also started an on-campus campaign where over 2,000 signatures were collected and sent to _____.

Here is an answer tip for Military Professionals:

- One of my greatest challenges as a military officer was when the Air Force reduced the size of our officer corps through a recent unplanned downsizing due to lack of economic funds. The Air Force reduced our forces by about 1,700 junior officer positions. I had to manage a team with greatly reduced staff.

Here is an answer tip for Medical majors:

- As a future medical doctor, this year's dominant challenge to us as physicians is to prepare for the unpredictable. The most important event recently introduced to us physicians, was a 27 percent reduction in Medicare reimbursements according to the Department of Health and Human Services. This cut has hampered resources from hospitals, to ancillary care, to even dialysis clinics. This problem is ongoing.

Here is an answer/suggestion tip for Teachers:

- One of the greatest challenges I encountered was preparing my students for the civics components of their EOC exams. I knew the students were not prepared thoroughly to take and pass this examination. I had to do rigorous teaching about the Constitution and the Amendments. I gave the students silly examples that related to Somerset Academy. I compared the U.S. president to the school principal and the Congress to the school's administration and laws to the school's rules about uniforms. This made learning fun and exciting for my students. My approach had to be simple but unique to get students engaged and ready for the test.

26. **What motivates you to be successful?**
This question helps recruiters to find out more about you as a person. Your answer can give them some insight into:

o   What makes you tick
o   What you enjoy doing and what you value
o   Whether you would do well in the job role
o   How you would fit into their team

When preparing to answer this question, you should think about:

o   What do you enjoy doing? Think about your course and your wider interests. What do they have in common?
o   What have you enjoyed while working at your part-time jobs or internships?
o   What sort of tasks are you best at? In what sort of environments (busy, deadline-driven, loud, quiet etc.) do you work the best?

Another suggestion tip:

•   **Example tip**: Use a few key words/attributes such as deadlines, results, opportunity, agenda, progress, work environment or money, innovation, recovery, advocacy, etc…then use a brief example to clarify.

Here is an answer tip for Mass Communication majors:

•   Deadlines motivate me. I am motivated by meeting set targets within set deadlines, as it gives me a sense of accomplishment and it's something that I can look back on and say, "I achieved that." I'm also motivated by visible results; for example, when I wrote an article for my student newspaper, I got a sense of accomplishment from knowing that up to 16,000 students would read it."

Here is an answer tip for Marine Biology majors:

- Opportunity and inspiration motivate me. As a marine biologist the sheer joy of figuring out how the ocean works is thrilling. You learn so many things ranging from tiny little plankton to giant whales, how they all interact with each other, with their environment and with people. I recall an experience working at __ (*share something important and the end result*).

Here is an answer tip for Healthcare majors:

- I am motivated by one word: "improvement." Being able to connect with the patient and actually help them with deal with their diagnosis and implement follow-up treatment is definitely very rewarding. I recalled treating a diabetic patient that was very concerned about her diagnosis. A 90-minute consultation was scheduled; I reviewed her medical lifestyle and psychosocial status. I performed a foot exam, checked and recorded blood pressure and pulse. Before her discharge, I educated my patient about continuous glucose monitoring the she would receive to help improve her glycemic control (Taylor et al., 2016). I was impressed with her response to the treatment and how she regained quality of life within six months. This is what continues to motivate me.

Here is an answer tip for entry level Computer Network Support Specialist:

- Efficiency motivates me. In the IT arena, change is constant and being able to adapt is essential. We are in an age where technology is moving at a speed of light and we are creating a new future. During my internship at *AT&T (name the organization)*, I had to test and evaluate existing network systems, perform regular maintenance to ensure that networks operated correctly, train users to work with new computer hardware and software and troubleshoot local area networks (LANs), wide area networks (WANs) and Internet systems (Bureau of Labor Statistics, 2015). As a result of my hard work I was awarded rookie of the month.

27. **What are the major reasons for your success?**
    This is not the time to become extremely self-centered and arrogant. Keep in mind that employers are often looking for team players rather than lone rangers. A good response to this question may relate to a mentor/and or work philosophy or the people you work with. Also, use this question as an opportunity to inquire about an appropriate "fit for success" with this company.

Here is an answer/suggestion tip:

- Success is when 10,000 hours of preparation meet with one moment of opportunity. Now explain how those hours have prepared you for a unique experience and what was the end result?

Here is an answer tip for Film Industry majors:

- I can honestly say my formula for success was failing in my first short film project while studying at Full Sail University. I think gave me good motivation to strive for true success. This is a very competitive field and I did not take the project seriously. The younger generations have lived practically their entire lives with the Internet and with wide access to increasingly interactive media, enabling them to understand the boundaries of what is possible with this form of the media; something that proved difficult for me. Being creative and original was the issue. I did not anticipate this and the film I created, *Cutting Edge*, didn't capture the concept I was trying to convey. Since then, I have worked on quite a few successful short films (*list a few of them*) and I am currently in collaboration with ___ to work on ___(Monster.com).

Here is an answer tip for Mentorship:

- Many years ago I learned an important lesson from Gwen Stewart, who was my professor, my first supervisor, and eventually, an important mentor. She told me her secret to success was to, "Look at each day as a new opportunity to be your very best. Set high goals, be honest, never say 'no,' and work with people who share your passion for doing their best." I've always remembered that advice and try to live it every day. I am very self-motivated, determined and honest. I really love what I do and I try to surround myself with people who share similar passions. I thrive in this type of environment.

28. **What are your assets, skills and strengths?**
    Employers need to take a bite out of your knowledge, experience and skills. This is not a question that you answer with mediocrity. This is a question where you can sell your resume.

    Here is the recommended formula; simply plug in your own information. You can answer this question many ways; one way is to break it up into the following:

Assets: Degrees, years in field, awards and selected accomplishments, research, publications, affiliations;

Skills: Lay out four strong skills and link them to the position for which you are applying;

Strengths: Jobs held and duties, etc.

Answer tip: Remember start with your academic background then transition into work experience.

1. I graduated from _____ (*institution*) and (*major/field*) with a B.A. or M.A. in _____ (major/field). I then matriculated to _____ (*institution, major/field*).

2. I have __ (#)_ solid years of experience, and __(#)___certifications in (*major/field*). I am a part of (*board/organization/affiliations*). I am (*state something unique about an award if it applies*)

3. After acquiring degrees from _____ (*institution*) __, I completed an exclusive internship at _____ (*fill in with name of internship program, such as:*

   Dental Internships Abroad in Spain...
   VA Corps Professional Internship Program (architecture)...
   Mayo Clinic Nursing Student Internship Program,
   FBI Honors Internships Program.

Note: State what you gained from the experience? Remember to connect what you have accomplished to the position you're applying....

4. I currently work at _____ as a _____my duties entail/selected accomplish ___ (lay out your duties thoroughly and then connect it back to the ideal applicant). Before then I worked as a _____ at ___ organization. My job duties entailed... (lay out what you have done clearly)

Here is an answer tip for Education majors:

• I started my academic career at Miami Dade College where I obtained my Associates in Arts degree with honors in special education. I then transferred to Union Institute & University in Cincinnati, Ohio, where I graduated *summa cum laude* with a Bachelor of Science degree in Education.

- In order to gain experience I did classroom observation at Meadowland Elementary School. I was part of their substitute teaching pool, participated in PTA events and tutored students in reading, language arts, writing and math. After five years I was hired at Spanish Lake Elementary School. Prior to that, I worked assisting pre-kindergarten through third grade students with general education. My responsibilities included translating lessons into learning experiences, evaluating students' academic and social growth, keeping records and preparing progress reports. The following year, I was promoted to a second grade teacher and continued to engage in teaching reading, language arts, social studies and ESOL.

- My duties include but were not limited to: maintaining standards of student behavior, identifying student needs, using of a variety of instructional strategies such as inquiry, group discussion, lecture, discovery, etc.

- The last school year I was given the opportunity to work as a SPED teacher, teaching mathematics, reading and language arts to a fourth grade class. As a SPED teacher, I provided written input regarding the student's goals, supplemental supports and accommodations/ modifications to case managers during evaluations and IEP, actively participated in IEP meetings, developed plans for effective communication, monitored and provided follow-up of students in inclusive classroom settings, provided crisis intervention, and assisted where ever there was a need.

- I am a certified prekindergarten and primary teacher, as well as a middle school English teacher. I possess an academic endorsement for ESOL and Exceptional Student education, and I am currently working on my American Sign Language Certification (Monster.com).

Here is an answer tip for Pharmaceutical majors:

- I graduated from Miami Dade College with my Associate of Arts degree in Biological Sciences; from there, I transferred to Florida International University's Honors Program to further my education. I successfully obtained a Bachelor's degree in Biological Sciences and then went to Xavier University for my Doctorate of Pharmacy degree. I currently work for Mount Sinai Hospital where I _____ (lay out duties clearly).

Here is an answer tip for Healthcare field:

- I am a highly motivated, hardworking and experienced professional with excellent skills in interpersonal communication, assessment, leadership and management. I recently graduated *summa cum laude* from the University of Miami with a Bachelor of Science in Nursing. I have two years of experience in the healthcare field.

- I possess several certifications that have helped me provide reliable and accurate care in the medical field; some of these include IV certification, Phlebotomy certification, EKG certification, CPR, BLS and ACLS certifications and other in-service skills such as OSHA, Infection Control. I am actually working at Jackson Long-Term Care as a Team Leader nurse where my job duties are administering injections, inserting catheters, operating equipment, managing a case load of more than 30 residents, solving problems, delegating, and administering medications and assessments.

- I have worked at several healthcare agencies where my duties included serving as a wound care specialist, planning and coordinating clinical requirements for staff, establishing treatment plans and ensuring that all Charting by Exception (CBE) is done with extreme caution. This is a gray area because CBE does not necessarily result in patient records having detailed information. Lack of detail could compromise patient safety, (Affinity Insurance Services, 2016). I also collaborated with managers to resolve issues to improve the work flow processes on current projects; and provided immediate support and education on policy, procedures, equipment and a resource using the four E's—engage, educate, execute, and evaluate.

- Lastly, some of strengths include educating my patient about their medication, providing rapid response time, solving problems, performing lab work and providing leadership abilities when asked to serve on a team (Monster.com).

29. **How have your technical skills been an asset?**
    Describe how you've used technical skills to solve a problem. Recall a problem, the skills you used to deal with it, and the successful results. This is a skill-detailed version of PAR (problem, action, results). Demonstrate how these same skills have been useful in other situations or in other jobs you've held.

Here is an answer tip for IT majors/professionals:

- My technical skills can be a tremendous asset to your organization. I am fully competent in Microsoft Office, Java and C++certified. I have a solid understanding of client/server, networking and Internet technologies fundamental. While working as a ____ (list your position) for ____ (name of the company). I researched and developed knowledge-base articles for Lotus Notes issues, resulting in an increase in first-call resolutions of 20 additional calls per week that saved company $57K annually. I exceeded issue-resolution targets and achieved exemplary customer satisfaction scores, consistently scoring between 95% and 100% on all calls (outperforming average of 90%). I also handled 30+ technical/mission-critical calls daily and consistently met high service standards. With this level of success I hope to continue with this organization (Monster.com).
- **Note**: Using statistics make sure they are accurate!

Here is an answer tip for Journalism majors:

- Although I never planned on a career as a writer or a publisher, much of my job in marketing depended on good writing and creative layout skills. Well, my part-time job with the Washington Post Newspaper taught me that, the changing media landscape and media consumption is continuous. While there I wrote brand-appropriate, creative pieces for a variety of mediums; both online and offline (i.e. sales aids, resource guides, iPad apps); I did some storytelling across various mediums; did some web writing and copy editing along with plenty research. I look forward to expanding my technical skill set here (Monster.com).

30. **How do you usually go about solving a problem?**
    The interviewer will want to hear the logic you use to solve problems as well as the outcomes you're able to achieve. Are you decisive? How do you narrow the options and make decisions? What do people say about your reasoning skills? What examples would they cite of your effective decision-making?

Here is an answer tip for Sign Language Interpreter:

- I look for these six things in every situation: who, what, when, where, why and how. Once I piece these areas together, I create a simple plan to execute a resolution to the matter. For example, I had to interpret in a college level math class, and the information was dense and math was not my subject. In signing the lessons, me and my team members used conceptual signs in order to clarify the meaning of the math. The signs that we used were intended to help students understand the important and subtle meanings of these abstract math concepts. When I was interpreting the information, I realized I shouldn't sign TIME as a clock and TABLE as an object that you put things on. I had to think about the application of the concepts. How would the student *use* the times table? ASL is a visual and active language. So in this case, I created a times table in the air as it appears on paper. It worked and the student was able to pass the class.

Here is an answer tip:

- It depends on the magnitude of the problem, but there is a basic formula I use that can be applied to any situation. When I need to solve a problem, I generally start by writing down as many ideas as I can. Next, I look for relationships among causes so I can group together symptoms of bigger problems. Usually, after I study these groups of problems, the best solution becomes readily apparent.

Here is an answer tip for Social Work majors:

- During my three-year tenure at the Department of Children and Families in Colorado, we had major issues with self-sufficiency transitions for older youths living with HIV/AIDS and who continued to be in the foster care system as adolescents. Approximately 20,000 to 25,000 youth age out the foster system annually (Child Welfare League of America, 2016). Due to unemployment and their lack of job skills, it was a major challenge helping these individuals gain self-sufficiency. I used a survey to find out what were the major issues and challenges facing these troubled youth. Once I found the common thread, I used that information to petition for more funding. I was able to secure funding from the Foster Care Independent Act, and was instrumental in securing federal funds to provide room and board to youth ages 18-21. Our department was also able to secure funding to help extend Medicaid up to age 21 through The Children's Health Insurance Program Reauthorization Act (CHIPRA). I was then able to provide transitional support programs to help our client's in their education and employment/career pursuit.

31. **Tell me about a time when there was no rule or precedent to help you attack a problem?**
Can you operate without structure? Describe your problem-solving process, especially the steps you took and the measures you established in a particularly trying situation. Demonstrate confidence and the willingness to take on more challenges.

Here is an answer tip for Entertainment Industry:

- I think one major issue in this industry is streaming. Streaming is rapidly becoming the dominant form of music consumption. It also pays artists the worst of any formats before it. In fact most consumers now attribute very little value to the recording itself, and most consumption (through YouTube, ad-supported piracy, or BitTorrent) happens at little-to-zero cost to the listener (Resnikoff, 2014). Since the primary model for compensating a music artists for streaming their music is to pay them per time their song is streamed we put a system in place to enforce this (be specific about the system that's in place). So every time a song is played, the artist gets x amount of money. Our team also implemented take-down notices and site blocking. We also issue our Popcorn Time Mitigation (PTM) service for broadcasters and content owners who want to prevent unauthorized rebroadcasts of their content via Popcorn Time (Haag, 2016).

32. **What's your greatest achievement to date?**
Be sure that the achievement you describe here is relevant to the job you're interviewing for. Also, be careful that your answer doesn't sound as if the best is behind you. Mention something great that you've achieved, but clearly communicate your belief that the best is yet to come.

Here is an answer tip for Scholarship Winners:

- One of my greatest achievements has been winning a full scholarship to attend Florida Atlantic University. This competitive scholarship required a lot of writing as well as 1,000 service learning hours to an organization that promoted intervention strategies. I completed my hours at (*name the facility*) ___ in (*state where it is located*)___. This organization provides (state the organization's main purpose or mission) ___.

Here is an answer tip:

- I played varsity basketball for four years and I'm proud to report I was still able to graduate with a solid GPA of ___. A lot of women on my team either took a reduced course load or let their grades suffer. I believe the reason I got through was sheer determination; I never ever let myself visualize anything but seeing my studies come to fruition within the given time-frame and with good grades. As a professional counselor, I continue to believe in the importance of a positive outlook.

33. **Tell me about something you accomplished that required discipline.** This is your opportunity to discuss a skill you developed, or a time when the quantity of work required solid time-management skills. How did you remain focused?

Here is an answer tip about Social Crisis Intervention:

- I have a child that has autism and I work as a part-time intervention crisis counselor while attending school full-time. I take it one day at a time. I receive family support and have developed a W.I.T. (whatever it takes) mentality, so I can finish on time and provide a better living for my son.

Here is an answer tip for Death in Family, Crisis, and Children:

- During my last two semesters of graduate school, I lost my mother to breast cancer. This was one of the darkest moments of my life. Additionally, I became a mother to my two younger siblings, who were 5 and 9 at the time, and I became parent too. So much was happening, but I had to buckle up and finish strong. I was living in dorms and had to take my sisters to school with me because I couldn't afford daycare. I had to get permission from their school to allow them to go to school three days a week. The other two days they would be in Boca Raton with me. Nevertheless, after those two grueling semesters, I finished my Communication Degree with honors and was hired by Miami Dade College, where I have been working ever since. I am now writing my first book, which takes much discipline.

Here is another answer tip:

- I had to work two jobs to put myself through graduate school. In addition, I did an internship at the *Washington Post* newspaper company while I studied journalism during the week, and on weekends, I volunteered at a shelter for _____. Juggling all these schedules was a challenge, but I did it because it was important to me to graduate without student loans.

34. **What is your greatest professional accomplishment to-date?**
    This is your opportunity to provide a concrete example that shows you are the ideal candidate for the position. Use an example relatable to your career. The goal is to highlight not only your past successes but also what you are capable of accomplishing if offered the job.

Here is an answer tip for Immigrants:

- One of my biggest accomplishments was being selected for the $30,000 annual Jack Kent Cooke Scholarship Award (2016). As a 21-year-old Nigerian immigrant, my parents struggled and gave up everything so I could have a brighter future. In light of the 276 young girls from my country that were abducted by the militant Islamic group, my parents were determined to have me come to the United States, where my dreams could be fulfilled. I think of the millions of talented individuals and students and wondered what makes *me* so special. My conclusion, in one word, I would say is, "Grace." Winning a full academic scholarship so my parents will never have to worry about how my tuition will be paid is a one-in-a-million Grace opportunity. I am glad I was the "one."

Here is an answer tip for Business/Graphic Design majors:

- My greatest accomplishment was making a significant impact on our company's meetings and webinar business. For example, with most businesses cutting back and hosting fewer events due to economic drawbacks, my creative team and I came up with a way to offer the same top notched experiences via webinars. Each webinar was accessible 24 hours a day and led by industry experts and company leaders. In the end we helped reduce the costs of event production by _____ percent and invested in more webinars worldwide. I hope to bring the same creativity and ingenuity to this establishment.

Here is an answer tip for Information Technology-Cyber Security Issue:

- I think one of my biggest accomplishments was working with a team to track down the Iranian hacking situation. Cyber security is a major issue we face today. These individuals were able to gain access by breaking through the security of a New York Dam.
  Our team learned that the breach came as hackers linked to the ____ government were attacking our bank websites due to very sensitive issues (Chiacu, 2015). However through our investigation we found out that this threat was for probing purposes. Our team was able to infiltrate and shut down their attempt. Our 24-hour cybersecurity information-sharing hub and an emergency response team coordinated responses to the threat to assess anything that might be critical to infrastructure. We immediately addressed the issue by providing "patches," "security updates," and "service packs". Secondly, access controls for networks were enforced by "firewalls" this helped restrict traffic to and from the network. Thirdly, a new encryption was enforced (Rowe, 2016). I take cyber warfare seriously.

35. **Why is service such an important issue?**
    The interviewer is trying to determine if the candidate understands the importance of customer service in establishing a positive image in the marketplace, and its impact on new business sales. Outstanding customer service is also a great help in establishing long-term clients and repeat business, the profitable company's "bread and butter." The longer the relationship, the greater the possibility of realizing a profit (gowrikumar. com).

Here is an answer tip for Healthcare Employees:

- I believe businesses can rise and fall on one word: service. Customer service is so important in the banking, teaching, social work, entertainment, and medical fields, just to name a few. When I volunteered at the VA Hospital, I noticed the level of customer service was inadequate. I'm aware that the Department of Veterans Affairs (2015) recently came under fire because a lack of service apparently led to the death of a patient. This should have never happened. I believe that it doesn't matter the field we pursue; providing quality customer service is a key to building a base of repeat customers, who are the backbone of most any business. We cannot afford to lose even one to poor quality customer service, particularly since it is costly and time-consuming to find and "recruit" new customers.

Here is an answer tip for Entrepreneurs:

- You know, word of mouth is still the best marketing tool. We are naturally drawn when a person gives rave reviews about a product or service. For instance, I recently completed writing my first book and needed to market it to college campuses. I volunteered to speak and provide free workshops to clubs and organizations, with one exception: instead of charging for my services, I would ask my clients to contribute toward my book. Well, it got off to a very slow start, and many times I questioned if I was doing the right thing. However, because individuals started using the tools, strategies and techniques I provide in my book I now have repeat customers. I also market to over 250 students per semester. I try to keep my product as fresh as possible in the minds of my customers so the message will attract and have a huge impact.

SUSTAINABILITY QUESTIONS AND ANSWERS

36. **Why is sustainability so important today?**
    Employers want to know about your ability to think outside the box. Sustainability is a hot topic discussion and could take on a variety of meanings. Sustainability may mean ensuring that natural resources are replaced or conserved for the long term and that ecosystems are not harmed. In terms of employment practices, sustainability may mean ensuring that employees are paid enough and given sufficient benefits to build families and contribute to their communities. Businesses are paying more attention to this issue because sustainable businesses are often the most innovative and they are constantly reviewing processes to find new solutions (co2australia, 2016).

Here is an answer tip for an Environmental/Business major:

- I believe everything we do has an element of sustainability in it-from climate change to energy to transportation to even waste management. For example, waste distribution is a great business opportunity, one driven by the continued increase of land fill tax and potential landfill bans. Most people think that the recycling industry consists of only a handful of community groups or their local curbside recycling program (California Integrated Waste Management Board, 2016). However, recycling is more than just collecting bottles and cans; in California alone, it's a multi-billion dollar industry comprised of diverse companies, large and small, engaged in a variety of activities. From what I have learned, your organization has been instrumental in the sustainability movement (Cawrecycles, 2016).

37. **Why is sustainability such an important issue for your career?**
    This is your opportunity to provide a concrete example that shows you are the ideal candidate for the position and how sustainability is essential to your career.

Here is an answer tip for Senior Engineering and/or Agriculture majors:

- I believe that sustainability is the most important issue businesses will face in the 21st century. I look at this issue not as a challenge but as an incredible opportunity. I am a recent graduate of the University of Wisconsin-Madison, where I majored in Sustainable Systems Engineer. During my tenure, I worked for Verizon, where we delivered solutions for the meteorological, geo-spatial and operational challenges facing the agriculture industry. With remote monitoring solutions, enabled by machine to machine technology and advanced cloud services, farmers were able to look at almost any data point that tells them when to plant, when to irrigate and when to harvest. Wireless technologies can even help them increase usable acreage for planting. I was able to observe this process and learned tremendously. -http://www.sensatrack.com/

38. **Describe a method you used to secure funding for sustainability projects.**

Here is an answer tip for Senior Oceanography/Biology/Business majors:

- I recently graduated from the College of Charleston where I participated in the organization called SIFE (Students in Free Enterprise, 2016). Our goals were to help cultivate and restore critical oyster beds. Unfortunately, overharvesting, habitat destruction, disease, nutrient excess from runoff and sedimentation issues are many of major problems affecting oysters' ability to repopulate naturally. So we first had to artificially create, feed and grow oyster larvae (Polis, 2013). My team and I were able to help produce one of the largest oyster hatcheries. Next, once the oysters were repopulated, it helped the reefs added an additional three million gallons of water filtration per day for the water of Ace Basin. Our organization was able to launch an oyster shell recycling program for Charleston-area restaurants. We used our business and marketing skills to prepare information and explain the program to restaurants owners in the downtown Charleston area. Ultimately, we succeeded in showing them how the ability to help replant and recycle oyster shells would help raise not only awareness but also significant funds towards efforts to create a better world for tomorrow (Webmaster, 2012)

39. **Describe a time when you implemented sustainability initiatives?**

Here is an answer tip for Mechanical Engineer/IT majors:

- While working for Miami Dade County Waste Management, I was part of a team that worked with representatives from ATT and Big Belly Solar to connect solar-powered, wireless public trashcans that recycle waste, compact trash and then notify an administrator when they're full. Already hundreds of locations across the country are using this new technology to reduce carbon emissions and to save money.

Here is an answer tip for Fashion majors:

- While attending Dallas Christian College *(Name of the college)* I participated in the World Wear Project (2016). I was a part of a team that work with representative from _____ *(list a few partners)* which help reduce the amount of textile products going into landfills. Through my research I found out that clothing and household textiles currently make up 5.2% of the waste stream (SMART Organization, 2016). We donated clothing to underprivileged communities and what we couldn't salvage we recycled them.

40. **How practical or pragmatic are you?**

Give the interviewer an example of some practical or sensible approach you've used to solve a problem. When was a simple solution the best solution? Had others overlooked the obvious? In this example, you'll want to show off your common sense skills rather than your academic skills.

Here is an answer tip for Business majors:

- Clean energy is increasingly sought after, and the demand placed on green energy businesses to provide reliable service is soaring. I recall when I worked for T-Mobile the remote machinery maintenance got shut down. Well, the complex and expensive repairs associated with remote locations and limited experts can be devastating to a business' bottom line. Our team did some research and we eventually partnered with Librestream. This organization helped streamline the troubleshooting process to remote field equipment and machinery. Using Librestream they were able to consult with experts in real time (Bentein, 2015). We utilized videos, voice images and onscreen drawing a field worker was able to share high-resolution video with the experts hundreds of miles away. This helped reduced response times in half, eliminated the cost of travel and allowed the teams to solve problems faster. I look forward to doing the same thing for this organization.

Here is an answer tip for Finance majors:

• I can usually pick up on an underlying problem, even if it's not too obvious. I recall an investment banker who visited our real-estate-finance class and asked us what might cause the Tokyo investment community a problem in attracting local investment dollars. A number of the finance students in the class started trying to think of some complicated reasons. I decided it would have to do with getting out of a bad market quickly, and that a non-liquid investment would create problems. I said investors would be unsettled if the primary investment is local real estate and inflation has caused the paper value to exaggerate the real street value. Obviously, that was the answer he was looking for. (Lindsay, K.R. 2006)

QUESTIONS AND ANSWERS ABOUT YOUR IDEAL CAREER

41. **Describe your ideal career.**
    Talk about what you enjoy, skills that are natural to you, realistic problems or opportunities you'd expect in this particular job or industry, and what you hope to learn from those experiences. Avoid mentioning specific time frames or job titles.

Here is an answer tip for Education majors:

• My ideal career matches my teaching philosophy. I believe that learning and teaching is a testament to the beauty that may be achieved by an active mind seeking to understand and assimilate experience, knowledge and action into our own matrixes. I try to relate my teaching principles to real life experiences. It is essential that educators move beyond the remote class room learning to provide service and hands-on experiences.

If our students are to compete with other nations they must be able to read, think critically, write proficiently and speak properly.

Here is another answer tip:

• I'd like to stay in a field related to training no matter what happens. I was too interested in business to work at a university, but I believe that teaching is somehow in my blood. I've been good at sales because I took the time to educate my clients. Now I look forward to training the new hires (Lindsay, 2006).

42. **Tell me something about yourself that I didn't know from reading your resume?**
   Don't just repeat what's on your resume. Think of a talent or skill that didn't quite fit into your employment history, but that's unique and reveals something intriguing about your personality or past experience.

Here is an answer tip:

• I like to dance and sing. I believe being able to express one's self in a variety of forms is important. The arts are crucial to our educational system and it's something I instill while working with Big Brothers and Big Sisters of America. The visual and performing arts also are essential to get into top schools such as Juilliard, New World School of Arts, etc.

Here is another answer tip:

• "I am an amateur photographer. The adage 'a picture is worth a thousand words' really does mean something. Taking photos and creating meaning are important. I think the visual arts are essential and bring out our creative sides." Then link your response to the position you are applying.

Here is another answer tip:

• "I've managed my own small portfolio since I was sixteen thus, the reason for my interest in investment sales. I've averaged a 12 percent return over the past eight years." You then link your response to the position you are applying.

Community Work Environment - Questions and Answers:

43. **Our company believes that employees should give back time to the community. How do you feel about this?**
    Describe a time you gave back to the community as a volunteer. Do you go above and beyond what's expected of you? Do you use your skills productively? Are you an unselfish team player? Demonstrate how your personal interests make you productive even when you aren't being paid.

Here is an answer tip for a Social Worker:

•   During my tenure at Florida International University, I participated in several community service activities, from planting trees and feeding the homeless to even volunteering with the Dress for Success organization. I was able to gain real-world experience and the skills I learned helped prepare me to work as a social worker; in fact, just learning about the many community organizations and resources that are available will help me in the social work field. Currently, I volunteer at Starfish Foster Home and this experience has been remarkable.

Here is an answer tip for a Pediatric Medicine volunteer:

•   My major is pediatric medicine. I thought that volunteering at Starfish Foster Home would be the perfect way to give back while gaining practical experience, even in a small way. I feed newborns, change their diapers, and also bathe and dress them. Sometimes, I even get to accompany some of the babies on their doctor visits. Securing a safe, nurturing and loving environment for these babies is the foundation of this foster care organization and I am happy to be a part of it.

Here is another answer tip:

•   I believe that in giving back, it returns to you. In my last job as a manager, I told each of my employees that they would be allowed to spend one Friday afternoon a month at a charity of their choice on company time, since Friday afternoons traditionally weren't as productive. Knowing they would be free to spend Friday afternoons donating their time to a charity, my employees worked harder and accomplished more in the mornings. For example, I spent my Friday afternoons contributing to an adult reading program. (Lindsay, 2006).

44. **To which types of community projects do you enjoy contributing your professional skills?**
    This interviewer wants to know if the candidate will be a good corporate citizen and what the candidate sees as his or her most helpful skills. Try to focus your answer on productive applications of your work-related skills. Don't get sidetracked describing a cause that doesn't demonstrate job-related skills. Avoid discussing any charity or organization that may be considered controversial.

Here is an answer tip for Marketing majors:

- As a marketing person, I've provided free advice and marketing suggestions to our local high school for its fund-raisers, as well as to a local real-estate office whose success is helping to raise my community's real-estate values.

Here is an answer tip for Communication Consultant

- As a communication consultant, I enjoy working with Professional Women's Group (PWG) program. I first got my start through the program by accident. I had an associate who was having a tough time taking care of herself and her children and through networking circles I came across this organization and signed up. My associate was able to get the help she needed and even received trained in basic technological skills. I now work with the Steps to Success Program, which focuses on employment skills, financial education and a professional image. I frequently volunteer my time to conduct training sessions, free of charge.

45. **What environments allow you to be especially effective?**
    Emphasize your flexibility and your ability to work in many different types of environments. Your answer should not consist of a "laundry list" of requirements (private office, few interruptions, and so on) or the interviewer may conclude that you will be difficult to satisfy.

Here is an answer tip Senior Ophthalmology/Business majors:

- I enjoy collaborative teamwork environments that allows for creativity, flexibility and discovery. The medical doctors that supervised our team really supported learning and "out of the box" research. I recently came back from South Africa where I performed my residency. During our team research we found out that 39 million in the world are blind and 80 percent of them are living in low income countries such as Kenya (World Health Organization, 2015).

- o We also discovered that people are going blind because of one single reason, lack of proper medical screening to catch certain diseases before the conditions worsen. The average eye exam runs about _____ without insurance. Its way to expensive and many can't afford it.

- o We created a funding organization and got major companies to donate based on the needs of the people. We were instrumental in getting local phone companies to buy in and help create a device that could help provide eye exams at an affordable price.

- o The result was an instant success because instead of _____, a single eye exam can be taken from a phone sent to medical institutions and could provide treatment. It's now a click away and only takes a persona on a bike with a smart phone, and $500.00 (cost of the phone). This was an unforgettable experience.

Here is another answer tip:

- Although I can work effectively in most environments, I prefer environments where people are their own bosses, within reason. I like to have a goal but be able to draw my own map to get there. To accomplish goals, I rely on asking questions and finding people receptive, so cooperation and access are important to me in a work group. (Lindsay, 2006)

QUESTIONS AND ANSWERS ABOUT CUSTOMERS

46. **Tell me about a time when you had to deal with an irate customer. How did you handle the situation?**
How you react when others lose their temper or become upset is very important in most positions, especially those in service industries. The interviewer will be looking for evidence of your aptitude for work that involves a great deal of contact with the public. Give an example of a time when you were faced with a difficult person and how you handled it. Your answer should illustrate your maturity, diplomacy and awareness of the needs and feelings of others.

Here is an answer tip for a Finance Major/Bank Teller:

• When I worked at Chase Bank, a customer came in and opened two accounts. One was a business account; and the other, a checking account. I explained the service fees to the customer and stressed the importance of having overdraft protection on each account. The customer refused my suggestion, and within three months, she incurred $60.00 in overdraft fees. The customer was irate but we were able to refund two of the fee charges. By compromising, I was able to keep our client satisfied, and retain her as a customer of the bank.

47. **Tell me about a customer service challenge you had to resolve; what happened?**

Here is an answer tip:

• I work for ___ (*name the company*) and a customer had a problem with a new piece of electronic equipment and called for assistance. I was the second representative to speak with this customer. The first technician our customer spoke with insisted that nothing was wrong with our company's equipment and that maybe she did something to cause a defect. The customer was in tears, saying one of our agents verbally abused her and when she asked to speak to the supervisor, the agent gave the customer the infamous two letter expletive and hung up. The customer called back, only this time, I was available to assist. I was able to resolve the equipment issue within a matter of minutes and decided to join my supervisor on the line. When I told the supervisor about the customer's previous experience, proper protocol was established. The supervisor was able to listen to the tapes from the call center, then fire the original technician, and promote me to a customer service supervisor position. It went from being the worst customer service experience ever to the best in less than half an hour.

48. **How do you handle a customer issue of being charged wrongfully?**

Here is an answer tip:

• Recently one of our customers stated there was a questionable change on his Citibank MasterCard from a vendor seeking to renew the customer's $400 membership. The customer expressed that the charge was done without his permission. I simply refunded the money and transferred our customer to the fraud investigation department. The pending card activity was canceled.

49. **What would you do if one of our competitors offered you a position?**
The interviewer is trying to determine whether the candidate is truly interested in the company, or whether he or she has chosen the company randomly.

Here is an answer tip for Insurance Sales:

• I would turn them down immediately. If the competition would stoop low and try to offer me a position, it shows the type of character they have. Besides, I am not interested in any other business or organization; I want to work for Geico. I believe in your motto, "15 minutes can save you 15 percent or more on car insurance" and as a valued customer myself for over ten years, I know I would be convincing selling your product to our local and global market.

50. **How do you manage stress in your daily work?**
It might be helpful here to describe a stressful project you've worked on and the specific actions you took to organize each step to see the project through. How did you keep yourself calm and professional under pressure?

Here is an answer tip:

• How I handle myself or keep calm and professional under pressure can be summed up with one word: "balance." I have found that a variety of factors can lead to stress, such as headaches, problems concentrating, low job dissatisfaction and low morale, just to name a few. First, I believe in pinpointing trigger mechanisms and becoming aware of them to help reduce stress. Second, knowing when to take a break is essential for the body re-energize. Third, I look for an outlet to avoid burn out. For instance, when I feel most stressed, I sometimes do the following: ___ (*name an outlet you use to avoid burn out*).

Here is an answer tip:

• Recently one of our customers stated there was a questionable change on his Citibank MasterCard from a vendor seeking to renew the customer's $400 membership. The customer expressed that the charge was done without his permission. I simply refunded the money and transferred our customer to the fraud investigation department. The pending card activity was canceled.

Here is another answer tip:

- Stress is a part of our lives and knowing how and where to channel it is important to reduce job burnout. I do three things:

  First - Set realistic goals. I work with colleagues and leaders to set realistic expectations and deadlines. I also set regular progress reviews and adjust my goals as needed.

  Second - Make a priority list. I prepare a list of tasks and rank them in order of priority. Throughout the day, I scan my master list and work on tasks in priority order.

  Third - Protect my time. For an especially important or difficult project, I block time to work on it without interruption.

51. **What do you expect to earn within five years?**
    Turn this question around and ask what's typical for the career path. Then consider, based on your skills and performance, the areas in which you're likely to excel. Leave it to the interviewer to name the appropriate time frames for promotions. Don't speculate, or you'll risk sounding arrogant and unrealistic.

Here is an answer tip:

- My expectation for the next five years is that my contributions will be recognized and appropriately rewarded. I realize that salary levels are based on a number of factors, including the company's profitability and the general business cycle that affects our industry, but I expect to take on greater responsibility each year and to be appropriately compensated for my efforts and contributions (Lindsay, 2006).

52. **How do you bounce back when things go wrong or not as planned?**
    Describe a time when some obstacle forced you to change your original plan, but you were still able to achieve the desired result.

Suggestion tip for all majors:

- First, seek clarity in the matter. Next, I evaluate three things – time, assessment and a goal formula – to help me when things are not going as expected. For example, I look at the time frame I have to make changes. Next, I assess whether adjustments need to be made in my plan of action. Finally, I try to make sure I remain completely focused on my goals, and that I don't get sidetracked.

Here is an answer tip for Education major:

- Communication is never easy when dealing with defiant students. During my service leaning experience at ___ (*name the high school*), I noticed two students that always challenged every task and assignment given to them. One day, one pointed out that I was their age so they couldn't really learn anything from me. I ignored the comment for a moment but soon addressed the matter because their verbal (and nonverbal) communication behavior was affecting the classroom environment. I insisted on an immediate audience with this student's parents and the matter was dealt with immediately.

Here is an answer tip for Law Enforcement major:

- Recently, I responded to a domestic violence situation where a three-month-old baby was at the center of the conflict. The father had a loaded weapon; the situation really got out of hand when he used the child as a shield. We found out that the armed individual had been in the system many times but suffered from a mental condition. He had been diagnosed with schizophrenia five years prior to this incident. The child he was holding was actually his brother, not his son. We had to get CIT (Crisis Intervention Team) involved (Watson and Fulambarker, 2016). Thanks to a thirty-hour training program I had previously attended, I knew what to do to diffuse the situation, remove the baby from harm's way, and disarm this man. The situation was intense but it ended on a good note.

53. **How do you manage your work week and make realistic deadlines?** To answer this question effectively, describe how you establish priorities, set deadlines, and determine schedules.

Here is an answer tip:

- I am a firm believer in the 80/20 rule. I tend to accomplish 80 percent of the work in 20 percent of the time. I ask for assistance with administrative or other time-consuming tasks so I can have the time needed to really focus on main issue. I always plan my own deadlines at least two days ahead of the given deadline. This gives me time to make the changes needed, as well as the opportunity to handle any unforeseen problems that may occur.

54. **What personal skill or work habit have you struggled to improve?**
Make sure you convince the interviewer that this particular work habit is no longer an obstacle.

Here is an answer tip for Fashion Industry majors:

- In this field nothing is the status quo, because the next big thing can be a catwalk or a campaign away. One of my greatest struggles is the talent pipeline. To quote Jean-Marc Bellaïche a partner at Boston Consulting Group (BCG), "One of the biggest challenges facing luxury and fashion companies today is finding, developing, and retaining great creative and business talent," I agree 100%. In fact, *The Business of Fashion Magazine (2015)* reported that 50 percent of respondents lack access to the best creative talent. So as a budding fashion professional networking is key for me. Working hard and exceling beyond my counterparts is vital to finding new and unique talent. Lastly, in order to attract unique talent there has to be an improvement of employer branding. I hope you will give me the opportunity to help create a brand to draw that next "big" talent.

Here is an answer tip for Education majors:

- Sometimes, I overanalyze things. I think I inadvertently give more to students and when they don't deliver it's a huge disappointment. I'm working on making students more responsible by doing the following things:
  o Strengthening and reinforcing the social contract.
  o Placing greater responsibility on the student.
  o Ensuring that students know that living up to their commitment to the social contract takes precedence over other behaviors (i.e., self-centered behaviors, etc.). This also means making sure they know that "a good game" or "an emotional hook" is not going to work to change the rules that are outlined by the social contract.

Here is an answer tip for Veterinarian majors:

- Well in this field a major struggle is unexpected outcomes that you will encounter. Arguably, euthanasia represents the most emotionally stressful situation for the vet (New Zealand Veterinarian Association, 2016). I remember my first euthanasia because it is such a distressing experience. At college, I learnt the procedures of how to euthanize an animal but had little training in how to deal with a distress client or my own grief. I learned that some things come with the job. I try not to beat myself up about it. Life is unpredictable and sometimes things won't turn out as you would like them to. I try to just accept it and maintain a healthy perspective.

Here is an answer tip for Social Work majors:

• I think one of the biggest things I have struggled with was having students age out of the foster care system and seeing their lives go down the drain afterwards. I have spent countless hours trying to be a mentor and to get them into programs that would help sustain them. However, I realized that letting the youths find their own way is necessary. I am not 100 percent there yet, but I am learning to let go, bit by bit.

Here is another answer tip:

• I had to learn to say "no." I used to be humble to the point that other staff members abused my kindness. Now, when I say "no," I offer to help by countering with something I'd like to do in return. This trade-off is more equitable and cooperation in our office improved over time. (Lindsay, 2006).

55. **Aren't you overqualified for this position?**
Emphasize skills and qualities such as critical thinking, trouble shooting, multitasking, etc., rather than the specific content of your degree. Sell your *desire, passion, drive* – that is, your *personal* qualities in conjunction with your professional and/or academic experience.

Here is an answer tip for Sustainable Career Professionals:

• Not at all, I believe that my skills and qualifications are a great match for your organization. I do have *(#??)* years of experience in the sustainability field where I started working as a student assistant for the Nicholas Institute Climate and Energy Program. I researched topics dealing with Clean Power Plan, greenhouse gas regulation under the Clean Air Act, the deployment of innovation energy technologies, state-level energy and environmental issues (Duke Nicholas Institute, 2016). It was a tremendous experience because the knowledge I gained through research far outweighed the learning in the classroom.

- Currently I work for University of Washington College of Environment and Forest Sciences. As you know there is growing concern among all sectors of society about meeting an ever-growing global appetite for energy. Well among the numerous alternative energy sources being explored today—is biofuel. Our research team wrote and received a $40 million Biofuel Grant from the US Department of Agriculture (USDA) to advance the science of biofuels.

- Our research focused on the commercial production of bio-based aviation, diesel, and gasoline fuels using cultivated poplars grown on tree farms. And a critical component of our work examined potential social and environmental impacts of biofuel production. We also knew that we had to expand our scope of research so multiple academic – both within and outside of UW – and industry partners participated in the work, leveraging a broad spectrum of expertise that allowed the project to dive deeper into numerous aspects of biofuel development, production, and commercial use (environment.uw.edu). I hope you grant me the chance to do the same for this great organization.

Here is an answer tip for Senior Business/Accounting Careers:

- I have my degree in __ and I have __ solid years in this line of work but more importantly the individual that will acquire this position needs to be able to self-sufficient, and that what I bring. Working for __ (name of company) I oversaw the department's finances; prepared projects and proposed budgets; reviewed project expenses; processed contracts and payment requests, and supported financial tracking. I bring all this to the table and more. I am interested in developing long term relations and expand my current responsibilities. I hope you will give me the opportunity to do so (Monster.com).

Here is another answer tip:

- My experience and qualifications help me do my job even better. For one thing, my good design skills will help to sell more books and my business experience will help me do my job in a more cost-efficient manner, thus saving the company money. Also, I'll be able to attract better freelance talent because of all my industry contacts. I feel that with me, you'll be getting a better return on your investment. Finally, I'm interested in establishing a long-term relationship with my employer, so you can be certain that if I do well, I hope I could grow with your company.

QUESTIONS CONCERNING VIOLATIONS, CONVICTIONS & TERMINATION

56. **Have you ever been convicted of a crime?**

Answering penetrating job interview questions is tough. Handling those that invade your privacy is even tougher. Employers sometimes ask questions that are "technically" improper (Jenks, 2016). Some of them don't realize what they are legally allowed to ask a job candidate. Being truthful is essential, especially since they will do a background check on you. It is unlawful for companies to ask, "Have you ever been arrested?" They may ask, "Have you ever been convicted of a crime?" Be real, honest, and tactful (Criminal Records and Employment, 2016).

Here is an answer tip for Ex-Offenders:

- I made some careless decisions/mistakes as an adolescent and headed down the wrong path. Growing up without a father, negative influences and little to no support opened doors that led to dead ends and I found myself in a place where no one would want to be. In retrospect, I take full responsibility for my choices and actions, and have been making every effort to steer troubled youth down a different path.
- In my spare time, I volunteer to speak at organizations geared to at-risk youth such as the Intercept Program, Children Youth and Families at Risk (CYFAR) Program, and the Boys and Girls Clubs (2016). I can honestly say the person I was is *not* the person you see before you today. I have had time to reflect on my choices and as American philosopher, psychologist, and educational reformer John Dewey once said, "Hunger not to have, but to be." My appetite has changed and so have my desires. I know I have not scratched the surface of my true potential and so this morning, I bring to the table the following:
  - o Excellent writing, editing, and oral communication skills.
  - o Strong computer skills including a high level of comfort with Microsoft Office (e.g., Outlook, Word, Excel, PowerPoint), web-based communications (e.g., Skype, GoToMeeting, etc.), and Internet research.
  - o High level of analytical thinking to solve problems.
  - o High level of knowledge and comfort with technology.
  - o A curious mind as well as an ability to ask the right questions and apply solutions to business problems (Monster.com).

57. **Have you ever been fired from a job?**

Getting fired, unfortunately, can happen to the best of us. It can happen even when it's not your fault. There could be a personality conflict between yourself and your supervisor. Your idea of what the job is going to be like might differ from what management was thinking. You could have simply messed up. It happens. You're not alone. Expert's estimate that at least 250,000 workers are illegally or unjustly fired (wrongful termination) each year and that's not counting those that were justifiably terminated (Doyle, 2015). Regardless of the circumstances, what should you do if you've been fired? Where do you go from here?

Suggestion Tip: Whether you were fired, terminated, laid off, let go, dismissed, downsized, or whatever…if you were fired…you may want to be up front about it, explain the circumstances and accept responsibility for your actions. For instance, what if you were fired because you decided not to compromise morals? Explain what happened.
- Also keep in mind the following:
  - o Don't blame
  - o Watch your posture
  - o Watch your tone as your answer this question
  - o Maintain eye-contact with the interviewer; don't shift your focus to the floor, walls, ceiling, etc.

Here is an answer tip:

- I was released after a major reorganization. The merging of different departments had caused a major change in the way things were done. There were some differences of opinion between my boss and I. In the end, I was relieved of my services. I take responsibility for my part in the way things turned out. I learned a lot from the experience, and in retrospect, I would have handled it differently. But that is behind me now, and I am ready to move on with a new perspective (Martin, 2013).

Here is another answer tip:

- Due to unclear office policies, I choose to pursue other opportunities. I believe that when you work in a professional environment certain information shouldn't be withheld from selected group of individuals.

Note: You might want to give a specific example of what information was being withheld.

Here is another answer tip:

- I became pregnant and my situation led to me being hospitalized. Eventually, I had used up my vacation time and unfortunately, had none left. Although I was an excellent worker, the organization couldn't hold my job for me. They terminated me three months after my pregnancy. I delivered a healthy, bouncing boy and now I am ready to start work again.

Here is another answer tip:

- As a working parent, I decided to return to school while working 40+ hours a week. This was taxing on my body and my mind. I managed both "careers" for a while but realized that I had to make a temporary decision that would lead to a permanent position. I worked less hours, accelerated my classes and finished my degree a year earlier than expected. It was the most difficult decision I had to make, but I am glad I did. Now I am ready to apply the skills and knowledge gained to your organization.

58. **Q: Have you ever been arrested other than for traffic violations?**

Here is another suggestion/answer tip:

- There's nothing I've ever done that would give your company any concern that I'd breach any trust that the job you have requires. (Some states allow questions about convictions, but not arrests. California forbids both. The interviewer may be concerned about employee dishonesty, hence the question. Your answer satisfies the concern without turning off the interviewer.) (Jenks, 2016)

QUESTIONS CONCERNING SPECIAL NEEDS POPULATIONS

59. **Tell me how you handled a crisis when working with children with special needs?**
    The interviewer is looking for an indication of the candidate's accountability and professional character. Describe a specific crisis, the cause and what you did to remedy the situation.

Here is an answer tip for Social Workers Majors-Autism Case:

- Well, I believe that working in this field is one of the most rewarding and when a crisis moment hits, I go through a mental assessment concerning four key things: triggers, strategies, procedures, and intervention. While working at CARD (Center for Autism and Related Disabilities, 2015), I remember I had a client age 13 and his environment changed within a matter of months. The client was use to his mother being within reach. We had to introduce him to another way of doing things. This was a major challenge because his support system was no longer in place. Based on the shows he would watch and our conversations, I had difficulties understanding how much information this nonverbal child was absorbing. Because of a change in routine and the mother not being able to cope, I had to reassess and incorporate a more "normal" routine (e.g., meals, play, and bedtime) into his new environment. I had to use a lot of storytelling to create new routines and behavior patterns. He is still adjusting and the results have been favorable. We were also able to get help for his mother and reunite them.

60. **What frustrates you in this line of work?**

This is another question designed to probe the candidate's professionalism. The interviewer will want reassurance that you are able to hold up under pressure. Describe how you've remained diplomatic, objective, or professional in a difficult situation.

Here is an answer tip:

- I wouldn't use the word "frustrated;" however, I have zero tolerance for the lack of care and concern that some show when working with special needs populations. I understand sometimes people may get burned out or stressed, but quality care is still the priority. I recall working or volunteering at ___ internship program (and maybe this was just an isolated case) and we had children that were visually, hearing and physically impaired. As you know, safety and mobility are some key concerns when working with these children. At the time, there was an impending hurricane and the evacuation procedure was not executed properly. Long story short, one of our clients ended up being left behind and there was a 10-minute delay. The management has since placed greater priority on training employees for better mobilizing and emergency evacuation.

61. **How do you make sure you meet the needs of a student with an IEP?**

Suggestion Tip:

- An IEP is an "individualized education plan." Students with special needs will be given an IEP, or a list of things that you must do when teaching the child. An IEP might include anything from "allow additional time for testing" to "needs all test questions read out loud" to "needs to use braille textbook." How do you ensure you're meeting the needs of a student with an IEP?

- First, read the IEP carefully. If you have questions, consult a special education teacher, counselor, or other staff member who can help you. Second, make sure you follow the requirements on the IEP word for word. When necessary you may be asked to attend a meeting in which you can make suggestions for updating the IEP. Finally your goal, and the goal of the IEP, is to make sure the student has whatever he or she needs to be successful in your class.

Here is an answer tip for Educator:

- I teach at Miami Gardens Elementary School and I had a 5th grade student who couldn't read or write at the grade level. I immediately scheduled a parent meeting to address the matter. I showed the parent the student's latest work and explained that I felt that the student's skills were not progressing at the appropriate rate for his grade level. At first, the parent didn't feel his son had any challenges and thought the child was just being lazy and didn't want to learn. I suggested he get his child tested immediately. Since we have an onsite psychologist, it made the testing process easy. We were able to diagnose that his son had a learning disability and then informed the parents of the student's options. We created an IEP tailor made to bring this student's level of learning up. With quarterly meetings and reinforcement of the IEP, the goal of reading and writing at a 5th grade level was met after a year. Although the student still struggles, by working together to support the child, there was tremendous progress.

62. **How has technology benefited students with learning disabilities?**
People with disabilities meet barriers of all types. However, technology is helping to overcome many of these barriers.

Here is an answer tip for Psychologists/Computer Educators:

• I recall that while working at Benjamin Banneker High School in Atlanta, Georgia as an assistant psychologist, I had a patient named Jose. He was a bright, talented junior with bipolar disorder and depression. That fall, he was beginning to have second thoughts about completing high school. His classroom work was often poor. His teachers believed that this was due to a lack of motivation. He talked about dropping out of school and was spending much of his out of school time with another youth who physically abused him, even shooting him with a BB gun.

However, in the spring, Jose enrolled in an elective computer class which covered basics of computer theory, hardware and web page design. After completing the class, he began talking about completing school and going on to college for a computer science degree. His classroom work improved and he is now searching for part-time jobs at computer stores. While he still struggles with his illness, Jose is now a student leader and often helps other students and even staff with computer problems. (2013, Project MEET).

Here is another answer tip for Educators:

• I recall interning at Luxury ADHD Treatment Center in Washington D.C. where I worked with a student named Tom. He was a bright, insightful high school student who had placement problems within traditional school settings. Tom was diagnosed with ADHD, conduct disorder, and there was also a question of undetermined learning disabilities and some problems with fine-motor skills. Typically, when presented with hand-written assignments or tests, he would spend a minimal amount of time with the material to be learned or the product to be generated. He would rush through his work, exerting minimal effort and turning in products full of mostly illegible, poorly organized, terse, one-word, and cryptic phrases.

However, when Tom was asked to demonstrate his knowledge or research results by creating a computer-generated product, he spent as much time accessing and processing the material as the teacher would allow. He was able to organize his work in a more sequenced and orderly format. He created answers using complete sentences, supported by evidentiary arguments. This was especially true if the product to be generated involved images and/or sounds as well. He spent days creating a PowerPoint presentation of his findings, insuring that there were perfect pictures to illustrate his points and providing bulleted lists of facts to further support his points. Tom asked many more questions to insure that he understood what was being asked of him and that he understood what he was discovering in his research. The end result was amazing. (2013, Project MEET).

Here is another answer tip for Elementary Teachers:

- Working at the Attention Center in Cleveland Ohio and Cleveland Elementary School I had a student named Eric. He was a ten-year-old with sensory motor integration problems and an ADHD/ bipolar disorder. He also demonstrated major problems with peer interactions. During his first month at school, recess became a problem and often resulted in major interventions by staff and even restraints. To both provide him a "recess" opportunity and to minimize peer interactions, we allowed him to put on earphones, listen to music, and explore educational Internet sites, and/or use social studies and other stand-alone software programs. Eric happily engaged in these tasks, thereby reducing the need for staff interventions and alleviating his own stress as well. As we develop his peer skills, we were able to reduce his time alone on the computer and/or use the computer as a vehicle for dyadic or triadic learning experiences. He is still making great progress. (2013, Project MEET).

QUESTIONS FOR SIGN LANGUAGE INTERPRETERS/DEAF COMMUNITY

63. **In your opinion, which country has the greatest challenge or need in this career field?**
    You must be an avid reader in your career field to properly answer this question. You don't need to know everything (I mean who does) but your response to this question will show if you are a well-rounded individual.

Here is an answer tip:

- I am from South Africa and I believe that there is an urgent need for sign language interpreters. About three-quarters of the deaf community is functionally illiterate and/or unemployed in my country, and only twelve schools exist for the deaf that offer elementary through high school education; furthermore, they all are concentrated in just three provinces. We have a major crisis concerning welfare, health care, financial and other support services for the deaf community (Annual Report, Republic of South Africa, 2013). In fact, training for ordinary day-to-day situations are still largely inaccessible to this population. Some problems are also experienced in the courts, at offices and even in hospitals where, due to the absence of sign language interpreters, injustices are committed against the deaf. Even in instances where interpreters are available, the standard of interpretation is unacceptable and therefore, aggravates the situation instead of alleviating it (National Consortium of Interpreter Education, 2009).

64. **What got you motivated to learn Sign Language?**

Here is an answer tip:

• Interestingly enough, I have several friends who are hearing impaired. My generation has grown up seeing American Sign Language on television shows and movies, and it really looks interesting. But I think my interest came in college when I had to provide service learning at a rehab facility. I noticed the interaction between the signer and the deaf patient. I liked the special care taken to make sure the patient was not being discriminated against.

Here is another answer tip:

• My son became deaf as a baby. He was born a month prematurely and had mucus in his ear. He was given a hearing test at birth and the doctors told us not to worry. A month after his birth, an otoacoustic emission test was required which measures the response of hair cells in the inner ear, and it came back normal (Children's Medical Center, 2016). But then we noticed Jermain began missing developmental milestones. He was slow to sit up, slow to stand, and slow to walk. I began to panic. He was given another test at 18 months and failed it. We noticed his hearing loss came later. My husband and I had to move quickly. He was recommended for cochlear implants and has been doing well ever since. I was thrown into something and never thought I would make it but I did. It was a real eye-opening situation for me. I know how helpless I felt at times, and now I want to empower others.

65. **What was it like learning sign language for the first time after growing up with an oral education?**

Here is an answer tip

- It was more of a gradual process of discovery. My mother was working as an oral interpreter in a public high school, and from the deaf kids there, she was exposed to sign language. She brought home sign language alphabet guides for me, then a sign language book (the ABC Book of Sign Language, I think). I vaguely recall trying to teach myself through that book. Then when I was 14, I took a sign language class at the local community college. After completing the course (at the time, the college didn't have any more advanced sign language classes) I had little if any sign language exposure until college (Burke, 2016).

66. **What is one of the greatest joys in this career field?**

Here is an answer tip:

- Where do I begin? Seeing the outcome of positive communication is one of the greatest joys for me. Knowing that the deaf community is being served and treated with dignity and respect is one of my greatest joys. I also love the opportunities this field provides for career development. For example, being able to participate in the School-to-Work program at the VRS (Video Relay Services) Interpreting Institute has given me firsthand knowledge in bridging the gap between the needs of the client and time delays in interpretation, because the relay services offer quicker turnaround time for issues to get resolved. I like how sign language video relay also minimizes the hang-up problem that frequently occurs with test relay services because of the more direct nature of a sign language relay call (Clymer, 2008).

Some Do's and Don'ts as a SLT

Do's	Don'ts
• Tap gently on his or her shoulder to get attention. • If beyond reach to tap, wave in the air until eye contact is established. • Switch lights on/off to get attention. • Establish a comfortable distance between you and the deaf person. • Establish eye contact before beginning communication. SASL is a visual language and therefore eyes are used to process the message. Eye contact is also used as a turn-taking technique, especially in group discussions. • Wait for your turn to start signing. • Keep your face clear of obstructions, e.g. hair, scarf. • Show that you are attentive by nodding slightly – if you are expressionless, it conveys inattentiveness.	• Do not touch elsewhere on the body, e.g. head, face, stomach or use a fist/punch or kick or throw things to get attention. • Do not stand before the light from a window. • Do not pass between two people signing - or excuse yourself if you have to pass by. • Do not stand too close. • Do not look away during the conversation, as that denotes termination of communication. • Do not sign with hands full of objects, e.g. cup, books. • Do not eat or chew anything while signing. • Do not stand in a dark spot.

Source: The ASL (American Sign Language Interpretation) http:// www.nidcd.nih.gov/ health/hearing/pages/asl.aspx

Off the Wall Questions:

There is no way to fully prepare for these types of questions or scenarios. These impromptu questions can make you trip, slip, fumble, and bumble! Don't get stumped but triumph. Interviewers want to gauge your priorities. Demonstrate poise, critical thinking, and yes, even a sense of humor quickly and make connections to your career. With these types of questions, Sarikas (2012) posits, "The interviewers are trying to catch a glimpse of the unrehearsed candidate in an unguarded moment."

67. **What would be the very first thing you would do if you won the lottery?** Whatever you do, ***don't*** say you would quit your job. It shows that you are not about being proactive or helping to connect with the community, investments, charitable organizations, etc.

Here is an answer tip:
* After I pay off all my debts and help family members, I would like to invest back in my alma mater, *(name the university or college you graduated from.* I also would provide a small portion of funds to go to students with disabilities. I appreciated the opportunity to work with these wonderful students when I was an intern saw firsthand the challenges the staff had due to budget cuts.

Here is another answer tip for a Social Worker major:

* I lived in Chicago and saw the tremendous impact violence and crime had on my community. I would provide funds to increase police visibility and safety programs for youth there, where some neighborhoods have the largest concentration of poverty and crime in America. Unfortunately, like some areas around the country, this city is plagued by intergenerational poverty, gang infestation, social disorders, economic plight, and the list goes on. Also, I would create a scholarship program for the best and the brightest students.

Here is another answer tip for an Environmental Studies major:

* I am from Brazil and while growing up clean drinking water was a scarce commodity. I was sick often due to contaminated drinking water. We had very little so now, given the opportunity, I am poised towards helping

provide cleaner drinking water to children and their families. I would also help provide more water filters in homes.

68. If you were a song or film, which would you choose, why?

Here is an answer tip for Music Business majors:

- I love oldies so the song would definitely have to be "We are the World." Michael Jackson and Lionel Richie wrote the song in response to famine that devastated the African Continent. The song raised $60 million for African Famine relief. It took the collaborative effort of countless singers, artists, and many other people to bring this project together. The song was re-launched in 2013 when the earthquake hit Haiti. We are powerful when we come together to help make the world a better place for those who are not able to do it themselves.

Here is an answer tip:

- I am a Christian so it would have to be "His Eyes in one the Sparrow." This song means despite hard times, times of uncertainty, and afflictions in our bodies, our Lord and Savior Jesus Christ watches over us. I remember when I lost my mother to breast cancer it was a dark period in my life. I was left to raise my two younger siblings (they still live with me today) who were age five and nine at the time. We went through terrible living circumstances, a shortage of food, and family conflicts but God kept us through it all. I sing this song with love from my mother and the hope she inspires in my life.

Here is an answer tip:

- I would choose to be the "Star Wars Film" for sure. I like the fact that a group of misfits work collaboratively to stop "The First Order". You have to be willing to work with other cultures in fact research from the American Productivity and Quality Center (APQC) (2015) repeatedly states that organizations succeed when they three things: 1. teach employees how and when to collaborate; 2. make collaboration part of people's jobs; 3. recognize and reward employees for collaboration. Applying these three initiatives creates a win/win situation for both the employer and employee. I also notice in the film that there seem to be a passing of the "torch" per say to the next generation who happens to be female. I like how the movie makes the point of including both genders. Hey may the force be with us.

69. **If you were a fruit, salad or food, which type would you be and why?**

You should choose a fruit that tastes good in a fruit salad along with many other fruits. Remember, think of how your response can provide insight into your chosen career.

Here is an answer tip:

- If I were to choose a fruit, it would be strawberries. They are delicious and provide a multitude of health benefits. Plus, they are colorful, bright, sweet, and tangy, and leave a wonderful lasting taste in your mouth!
  Note: You can link it even further to your career field using some practical work related information.

Here is another answer tip for Business majors:

- If I had to choose a vegetable that tastes good it would be the lettuce. I like how lettuce makes up the bulk and serves as the core aspect of the salad. As a business leader, I am at the center of everything. I understand that all eyes will be on me to perform well and having a strong foundation is vital to business success. Salad also blends well and can be added to any type of meal. So, like lettuce, I am able to adapt and "go with the flow" seamlessly.

Here is another answer tip for Nutrition/Physical Education majors:

- According to the CDC, over two-thirds of Americans are obsessed with what to eat. As a nutrition/health science major I believe that foods high in fiber are the way to go.
  As a P.E. teacher the exercise regimen for many of our students is very poor. I would give incentives to students to promote healthy life styles. I would have my students practice better eating habit at least three time a week, and have them report of their individual progress. Besides, I agree with the Michelle Obama's slogan "Let's Move", for combating the obesity epidemic within our nation is so important.

Here is another answer tip for Fashion Industry majors:

- I would be grapes because it comes in clusters and connects to a vine. Being able to connect and network is a must in this line of work you can't do it all by yourself.
- **Note**: You can link it even further to your career field using some practical work related information.

70. **If you were a utensil, which would you be and why?**

Here is an answer tip:

- I would be a Spork – a combination of a spoon and a fork. It shows versatility and has the added benefit of holding more than the average utensil. Working in any career you have to be able to multitask. You have to have a high aptitude and assist when needed, follow detailed instructions and not miss important details.

71. **If you were bitten by a zombie, what would you do?**

Here is an answer tip for Physician Assistant majors:

- Amputate the area to prevent further infection. As a physician assistant, we have to assess patients properly and follow the doctor's recommendation on the proper course of action and in order to save the patient (or in this case, my life!). I would look for other remedies but if amputation is the best route, then it should be taken expeditiously.

Here is an answer tip for Computer Programming majors:

- As a computer programmer, virus prevention is the first priority. For instance, if your computer has contracted viruses such as "Goner," "Trojan Spy," "Rootkit," "Love Bug," and/or "Code Red," this needs to be dealt with swiftly. These viruses have wreaked havoc on millions of people across the globe. To safeguard against the ever increasing swarms of viruses, I would recommend that proper precautions be in place in a timely manner. I would quarantine immediately to prevent their further spread and locate the source.

72. **If you were a medicine, which would you be and why?**

Here is an answer tip for Healthcare majors:

- I would be penicillin. It was an accidental discovery over 86 years ago, but it has changed the course of medicine ever since. Penicillin helped reduce the number of deaths and amputations of troops during World War II, and has enabled physicians to treat formerly severe and life-threatening illnesses such as bacterial endocarditis, meningitis, gonorrhea and syphilis, just to name a few (history.com). This antibiotic still saves lives today.

73. **If you went through a machine as a dime and you came out a quarter, what just happened?**

Here is a suggestion tip:

- Talk about change, increase, or profit. In the business field, for example, the word "profit" is vital in order for a business to thrive.

Here is an answer tip:

- One way to make a profit is by cutting cost. As an graduate student I worked at _____ *(name of organization)* and the company had an entire building of 100 IT engineers tasked with maintaining its primary application. The total yearly cost to maintain this team was into the millions. So management decided to outsources almost all of our IT. We leverage Cloud computing via several cloud providers. The result is that we have more processing power, more bandwidth, a higher level of redundancy, and the same 24 x 7 operational control and, get this: higher up-time. Now our profit margins are far lower as a result (Stringfellow, 2015). I hope I get the opportunity to show you this same level of service here.

74. **Which sustainable product would you use to display and why?**

Here is an answer tip:
- I would be a fabric that is hypoallergenic, constantly worn, durable, organic with natural fibers and some man-made materials from renewable resources. I would be the fabric in handcrafted, vintage, 'smart clothing.'

75. **If you were a land or a marine animal, which would you be and why?**

Note: Choose the most efficient animal and connect it to your work ethic.

Here are some suggestion tips:

- I would be an **Octopus** because I have really learned to multitask in
  _____ (*your career field*) without reducing the quality of my work.
  (Elaborate on a few things).

- I would be a **Salmon** because in the __ (*your career field*) arena you
  have to know where the next big move will take place. Salmon have to
  swim upstream which is a daunting task, survive hungry bears and other
  wildlife predators just to hatch the next generation. The next generation
  of innovators in my field must be able to handle the challenges and
  know how to maneuver effectively. I remember my internship at MGM
  Studios... (Elaborate on a few things that show the interviewer how you
  "swam upstream" and handled difficult challenges).

- I would be an **American Bald Eagle** because of three main reasons:
  First, they have keen eye sight. As a crime scene investigator, I have
  an eye for spotting evidence, and am able to zero in on minute details
  that can make or break a case. Second, their nests are located at the
  top of mountains and trees. In this field, quality and excellence are
  never compromised. Third, the mates work together to build the nest
  and raise their off spring. In this career field it is a must to have strong
  interpersonal communication and teamwork skills. A person must be able
  to understand, work with, and show respect for different perspectives. I
  remember my internship at Microsoft... (Elaborate further with specific
  practical work related information).

- I would be a **Peacock** because in the fashion industry beauty, grace and
  style are the hallmarks to becoming a brand or being the next major
  trend. I remember my internship at Betsy Johnson... (Elaborate further
  with specific practical work related information).

- I would be a **Chameleon** because in this industry you have to be versatile
  and adaptable. It's also important to go with changes and be open to new
  approaches. I remember my internship at the Apple Store... (Elaborate
  on how you were versatile, adaptable, and open to new approaches while
  working there).

76. **If you were a superhero, who would you be and why?**

Here is a suggestion tip:

- **Batman** - I would prefer to be a superhero like **Batman,** who doesn't have superpowers per se, but who **relies on his intelligence** and use of the **right tools to get the job done**. As a law enforcement professional I often have to... Note: You can link it even further to your career field using some practical work related information.

Here is a suggestion tip:

- **Ironman** - connects to Teachers/Technology...who use physics, science, and math is a visionary who promotes creativity. **Note**: You can link it even further to your career field using some practical work related information.

Here is a suggestion tip:

- **Fantastic Four** - connects to Education, Engineer, Health Science Major- The character name "Reed" enjoys...math, and chemistry... nurses/engineers need strong foundation in these areas. **Note**: You can link it even further to your career field using some practical work related information.

Here is a suggestion tip:

- **Aqua Man** - connects to Marine Biology/Biology majors...environment, botany, sustainability etc.... (Elaborate on a few things). **Note**: You can link it even further to your career field using some practical work related information.

Here is a suggestion tip:

- **Super-Man & Spider-Man** - connects to Journalism majors...great writers, follow the story, writes for the Daily Bugle etc. he uses his investigation, problem-solving skills to find the suspects and bring them to justice...(Elaborate on a few things). **Note**: You can link it even further to your career field using some practical work related information.

Here is a suggestion tip:

• **The Beast-** connects to International Relations major because not only is he a great speaker and team player but his role is unique in that he works with foreign relations and tries to bring ___ to both humans and "mute tins" alike. (Elaborate on a few things). **Note**: You can link it even further to your career field using some practical work related information.

Here is a suggestion tip:

• **Mystique-**connects to Marketing, Business and International Relations majors because she is able to adapt perfectly to her environment. People who are not able to adapt get stressed and lose interest quickly on a job. You do not want that to happen to you. Kokemuller (2014) reported *that r*esults of an employer study presented in December 2011 by the Accrediting Council for Independent Colleges and Schools revealed that fewer than 10 percent of employers felt colleges were adequately preparing students for career success. Employers indicated specifically that employees performed below expectations on adaptability and the closely related skill of critical thinking. **Note**: You can link it even further to your career field using some practical work related information.

Here is another suggestion tip:

• **Wolverine-**has adamantine steal this connects to law enforcement and business majors. In this field you have to be resilient and able to bounce back from anything. A person must also create an environment of interdependence and strong leadership is the driving force behind it. Wolverine is able to lead while at the same time create new pathways for a sustainable future.

77. **Why should we hire you? What sets you apart from the other candidates?**

Do not be distracted by the mention of other candidates; you don't know anything about them and they could be fictitious. Focus on what strengths you bring to the table. These should be consistent with the four things most employers are looking for in candidates during the job interview: **competence, professionalism, enthusiasm**, and **likability**. Remember, they are looking for chemistry between you and them. Be prepared to summarize in 60 seconds why you are the best candidate for the job.

Here is a suggestion tip: Ask what they require in the ideal candidate and share how you either meet their qualifications or exceed them. Limit it to three key strong points. Here is a way to **tackle** this question.

- o First, the ideal candidate must be certified. I possess certifications in… (list a few).
- o Second, the ideal candidate should have a great deal of experience. I bring _(#)_ years…
- o Finally, the ideal candidate must be able to work in __ environment….must possess skills in…
- o Now as far as what sets me apart from the others… (Note: Consider tying this to the company's mission, vision or slogan). The leave them with something strong to remember you.

ACRONYMS are a great way to close off; remember, the interviewer has asked: **What sets you apart from others?** Briefly recap your skills, experience, humanistic side, and so forth. The key is to leave your interviewer with a strong impactful statement.

W.H.I.P	S.H.A.R.P.	S.T.A.R.	L.E.A.D.E.R.
C.A.K.E.	P.I.E.	N.U.R.S.E.	C.C.C.
5 P's	T.O.P.	H.O.P.E.	S.K.I.L.L.E.D.
G.O.A.L.	3 S's	T.E.A.C.H	3 T's
L.A.W.	S.M.I.L.E.S.	C.H.A.N.G.E.	3 A's

Here is an answer tip:

- During my research about your organization, I learned three principal reasons that explain why I should be hired for the RN position in your company. First, **I have the right academic preparation**. You mentioned that the suitable candidate must be a graduate from an accredited school of nursing with current R.N. license. In January 2014, I obtained my Bachelor in Science of Nursing degree and graduated *summa cum laude* from the University of Miami, one of the best nursing schools in Florida, which is also affiliated with Jackson Memorial Hospital. While there, I completed a clinical rotation on all the units.
- Second, **I have the right certifications and credentials.** You mentioned that the successful candidate must have current Basic Life Support

and Advanced Cardio Vascular Life Support Certifications from The American Heart Association; I have both of these.

- Third, **I have the right skill set to be successful in this job**. You mentioned that the chosen candidate must have excellent written and verbal communication skills, which I possess. This requirement is one of the most important skills because nurses may write case studies, lab reports or research findings, depending on what area of nursing they work in. It's also important for nurses to have technical writing skills, the ability to research and analyze treatments and processes, and to share this information with their peers – all of which I also have done. In addition, I am multilingual (English, Spanish, French, and Creole) and have experience in various settings, such as clinical, geriatrics, and triage. For these reasons and more, I believe I am a strong candidate for this position.

Note: *Remember your response doesn't have to be this lengthy.*

What sets you apart from the other candidates?

- Your company's slogan, "The Heart of Your Health," and mission to revolutionize healthcare services nationwide, equates perfectly with my philosophy. As a nurse, I will make a difference and build on quality leadership, care and expertise. In the heart of everything is a good leader and in this field you need nurses who are not only highly skilled caregivers but also strong leaders.

  - **L - Listen**. It's important to listen to what the patients' needs are in order to provide the best quality and timely care.
  - **E- Educate**. Education is a priority for the patients to know about their options, treatments and precautions to follow. Continuing education for staff is also critical.
  - **A - Advocate**. One of my priorities is to advocate for patients when they have nobody to help them when seeking care.
  - **D - Delegate**. Delegating the right tasks to the right people is one of my skills as a team leader.
  - **E - Experienced**. I'm an experienced nurse who knows the field and who knows what adequate care means according to AHCA (spell out the full name of this organization).
  - **R – Resolve**. I resolve issues quickly. Conflict resolution is one of my strengths. I have had to manage relationships between patients, family members and staff members. I am asking you to give me

this opportunity to share what I have learned and help you continue in your mission.

Here is another example tip:
Note: Simply fill in the blanks

* As I reviewed your qualifications three key things stood out concerning your ideal candidate. First you ask for someone to be _____, I am certified in ___ and ___. Secondly, you are looking for someone who is ___. I have repeated through this interview that while working for ___ I had to_____ and ___. Thirdly, you are asking for someone with ___. I bring this quality because being recognized for _____, I was able to _____.

What set you apart from the other candidates?

* What separates me from the other candidates is wrapped up in your slogan, "With you every S.T.E.P. of the way." This equates perfectly with my own philosophy. To me S.T.E.P. means:
S - Standards. As an educator it's important to set and maintain high standards in the learning environment. By creating a fun, yet creative learning environment, students will be motivated to excel.
T - Time and Testing. I have to give my students sufficient time to master the skills taught in the classroom. I do this through group presentations, mock cases and written essays. In addition, it is essential for our students to be able to compete on a global scale. This can only happen through proper testing methods.
E - Enrichment. Enrichment does two things: (1) It keeps advanced students engaged and supports their accelerated academic needs; (2) It provides opportunities for students to pursue learning in their own areas of interest and strengths (Handbook for Gifted Education, 2015).
P - Passing. Good teaching is critical to helping students pass the content area and the course. Making sure our students don't drop, repeat or fail should be our number #1 priority.

Questions and Answers about Salary:

Let's face it, when it comes to "the money" question, most applicants squirm and most companies want to hire you as little as possible. Make sure you are realistic and honest about what you expect and do your homework.

78. **We can't pay you what you are truly worth.**

Here is an answer tip:

- Truly I understand that with an unstable economy no one can afford to pay their employees their truth worth. However, I am willing to work for __, because I know your company will improve and so my starting salary will not be a permanent thing.

79. **How much do you expect to get paid?**

Here is an answer tip:

- All Healthcare (2016) says a good way to answer this questions is the following, "I'm more interested in the role of ____ itself than the pay. That said, I would expect to be paid the appropriate range for this role, based on my __ years of experience. I also think a fair salary would bear in mind the high cost of living here in New York City" (this last statement depends on where you reside).

Here is an answer tip:

- Well, based on my research the average salary for this position is between *X* and *Z*, and based on my _(#)_ year (s) of experience, I would like to negotiate within this range.

80. **We are having budget cuts and unfortunately we can't offer you a raise now.**

Suggestion tip:

- Know about the budget cuts in advance, so you won't be surprised. Check out *salary.com* to get an idea about the pay range for your desired position.

Chapter 4

RESUMES, COVER & THANK YOU LETTERS

"The resume focuses on you and the past.
The cover letter focuses on the employer and the future.
Tell the hiring professional what you can do to benefit the
organization in the future."
-Joyce Lain Kennedy

YOUR COVER LETTER

The cover letter serves as a Sales Pitch, an Appetizer and an Entree.

It should address four things:

1. Company Motto= **Attention/Purpose**
2. Skills/Work Ethic= **Arouse Interest**
3. Experience= **Desire**
4. Press for the interview= **Suggest Action**

SOME TIPS TO THINK ABOUT:

1. Personalize the letter **ONLY** if you know the name of the hiring authority.. If you are not sure, this is what you say:
   Attention: Hiring Manger or Attention Search Committee or Attention Human Resource Department or Attention: Dean Stewart, Director of Sales and Marketing
2. **Be natural. K.I.S.S. (Keep It Simple Sweet)** Use simple, uncomplicated language. Don't try to sound like someone else, particularly if that means using unnaturally formal language, convoluted sentences, and words you have never used before (perhaps missing them in the process).
3. **Be specific and get to the point**. Your cover letter should be intriguing enough to get the reader to look at the resume. List a few of your skills and qualification. Remember this is an introduction to the resume. Make sure you answer the question, "Why should they hire me?"
4. Use bond/resume paper, be positive, polite, professional, and proofread and do not forget to **sign it.**

THE COVER LETTER

Date
Name ————————————————————
Title ————————————————————
Organization ———————————————
Address ——————————————————
City, State, Zip Code ————————————

Attention Mr./Ms. Last Name (Job title):

First Paragraph/Mention their mission: Why you are writing. Remember to include the name of a mutual contact, if you have one. Be clear and concise regarding your request.

Middle Paragraphs: What You Have to Offer. Convince the readers that they should grant the interview or appointment you requested in the first paragraph. List your degrees/skills/qualifications. Make connections between your abilities and their needs or your need for information and their ability to provide it.

Final Paragraph: How You Will Follow Up. Remember, it is your responsibility to follow-up; this relates to your job search. State that you will do so and provide the professional courtesy of indicating when (one week's time is typical).

Sincerely,

Your Signature

Your Typed Name

COVER LETTER PRACTICE

Date

Name
Title
Organization
Address
City, State, Zip Code

Attention Mr./Ms. Last Name (title):

First Paragraph/mission: Why You Are Writing. Remember to include the name of a mutual contact, if you have one. Be clear and concise regarding your request. Connect with their mission, vision or goals.

_____

_____

_____

Middle Paragraphs: What You Have to Offer. Convince the readers that they should grant the interview or appointment you requested in the first paragraph. **List your degrees/skills/qualifications. Make connections between your abilities and their needs** or your need for information and their ability to provide it.

_____

_____

_____

Final Paragraph: How You Will Follow Up. Remember, it is your responsibility to follow-up; this relates to your job search. State that you will do so and provide the professional courtesy of indicating when (one week's time is typical).

_____

_____

_____

Respectfully,
Your Signature

SAMPLE COVER LETTER CIVIL ENGINEER

Name, address & email

Date

Attention Human Source:

I respectfully submit this cover letter and resume for the position of Civil Engineer.

The Better Opportunity Lending National Corporation (BOLNC) was first created in order to assist citizens with their finances and building their dream retirement homes by offering quality services.

I currently hold a Master's Degree in Civil Engineering and Architecture from the Massachusetts Institute of Technology (MIT) as well as in Interior Design from the New York School of Interior Design. For the past three years I have been working in White Rock Quarries as Head Supervisor and Civil Engineer. There my job duties entail training new employees in OSHA safety procedures and daily work routines and evaluating and reviewing projects for quality and completion. Some of my qualifications include:

- Certified PE Civil Engineer
- Certified Architect
- Certified Interior Designer
- Outstanding Communication Skills
- Problem Solving and Critical Thinking Skills
- Experienced in AutoCAD
- Heavy-duty Equipment Specialist

In addition to the qualifications above, I am OSHA certified and multilingual. I have worked as the Interior Design Manager at Skidmore, Owings & Merrill for three years where I was the assistant to the division head. Some of my job duties included compiling job specs and supervising tendering procedures, resolving design and development problems, managing budgets and project resources, scheduling material and equipment purchases and deliveries, making sure the project complies with legal requirements, assess the sustainability and environmental impact of projects.

I have received numerous awards throughout my career such as earning the High Customer Satisfaction Award and becoming the winner of the Outstanding Projects and Leaders (OPAL) Award for Interior Design.

During the course of my twelve years in this field, I am confident I have gained the expertise and experience necessary to be an asset to your corporation. I believe that given the opportunity I can make a tremendous contribution to your firm as I have done in the firms prior. I would appreciate meeting with you to discuss your future goals and mutual objectives.

Thank you in advance,

Name & Signature

SAMPLE COVER LETTER

PARALEGAL ASSISTANT

Name, address & email

Date

Attention Director of Human Resources,

I respectfully submit this cover letter and resume for the position of Paralegal Assistant.

When LRFJ Corp, started in 2006, your main purpose was "to provide a legal justification in defense of our representative and continue to serve to the at most power of our abilities" by using personnel that were experts in their fields.

I currently hold a Bachelor's degree in Intellectual Property Law from one of the most prestigious universities of the nation, University of Miami. I also have two Associate's degrees in Pre-Law and Paralegal Studies. For over nine years I have worked as a Legal Officer onboard 2 different submarines and 1 major command that consisted of more than 1,500 personnel. Some of my qualifications include:

- Florida Registered Paralegal
- Solid Communication Skills
- Legal Correspondences
- Legal Research
- Notary Public
- Analytical and Organizational skills
- Fluent in Spanish and English

In addition to the above, I have also worked as a Law Clerk for the 11th Judicial Circuit of Florida, the largest trial court in the state, which required for me to a lot of drafting of legal documents such as witness statements and court orders. I have received numerous awards throughout my career such as being awarded the Administration Professional of the Year, selected as the #1 Sailor in the entire command three years in a row.

Since I have gained the knowledge and experience throughout my years in this field, I am positive I will be an asset to your Corporation. I believe with a given opportunity I can demonstrate to you that together we can provide the justice that every member of society deserves. I would appreciate meeting with you to discuss our goals and our mutual objectives.

Thank you in advance,

Name/Title/Signature

SAMPLE COVER LETTER

REGISTERED NURSE

Name, address & email

Date

Dear Allied Medical Staffing,

I am writing this letter in anticipation of joining your esteemed organization as a 'Registered Nurse' as advertised.

When this organization was established in 1982, the mission that differentiated this organization from other companies is the passion, excelling motivation and the enthusiasm towards your patients and profession. My skill sets will be helpful in meeting your organizational goals.

I am an experienced health care professional, working as a Registered Nurse for the past 7 years. I received my BSN degree in Nursing from the University of South Florida in 2005 and worked as an intern at Jackson Memorial Hospital for four years, consistently receiving outstanding evaluations. Also I hold a Master's of Science in Nursing from the University of Miami and currently working at the University of Miami Hospital. I am sure my extensive knowledge and experience, qualify me as the ideal candidate for the position.

I strive to give the best possible quality nursing care for my patients with optimum utilization of all the available resources. My prolonged period in the industry has imbibed in me the ability to integrate with patients on a personal level and make their stay as comfortable as possible. I would like to schedule an appointment with you to further review my qualifications and experience, and discuss how I might contribute to the ongoing tradition of excellence at Allied Medical Staffing.

Thanking you for your time and consideration.

Sincerely,

Thank you in advance, (Name/Title/Signature)

SAMPLE COVER LETTER

COMPUTER ARTS ANIMATION

Name, address & email

Date

Attention Human Resources:

I respectfully submit this cover letter and resume for the Computer Arts/ Animation position.

When Vivid Creations started your main purposes are to create and display the best productions applying the combined skills, talents, and proficiencies of your projects to bring more clients to you. As well as, using creative production methods to create high-end results with limited budgets. Also, using state-of-the-art equipment to bring out your projects maximum potential while promoting active learning, critical thinking, and engineering judgment, coupled with business and entrepreneurial skills.

I currently hold an Associate's Degree in Computer Arts & Animation from Miami Dade College. Additionally, I have a Bachelor's degree in Game Development & Design from Full Sail University. For the past three years I have worked at RIOT Games as a character designer/developer designing characters for their successful game "League of Legends." Some of my qualifications include:

- Adobe Certified, Microsoft Office Certified
- Knowledgeable in most 3D programs such as: Maya, 3Ds Max, Unity, Cinema 4D
- Knowledgeable in CSS/HTML and C++ & Java Programming
- Exceptional Communication Skills

In addition to the above, I have also worked as a Web Designer for ICE Portal and as a Cashier for a well-known retail store, The Home Depot. I have received a good amount of recognition and some awards throughout my career such as being part of Full Sail's Hall of Fame for helping design some of the character concepts of "Wreck It Ralph" and "Frozen" for Disney. I have gained the knowledge and experience necessary to be a great asset to your firm. Given the opportunity, I can make a tremendous impact on the success of your organization. I would appreciate meeting with you to discuss your goal and mutual objectives.

Thank you in advance

Name & Signature

SAMPLE COVER LETTER MUSIC BUSINESS

Name, address & email

Attention Search Committee:

I respectfully submit this cover letter and resume for the position of Music Business Manager.

When Promising Future Agency started, your main objective was to link employers and employees to establish economic growth. As a No. 2 "Most Employment Satisfaction in America" agency, and a "Best Customer Experience Center", I know your priorities are well structured and aimed at achieving your strong commitment to providing promising services.

I currently hold a Master's degree in Contemporary Performance from Berkeley School of Music, as well as a Bachelor's degree in Show Production and an Associate degree in Music Business. For the past five years I have worked as an Artists and Repertoire (A&R) representative as well as the head of the A&R department of Island Def Jam Music Group. Some of my qualifications include:

- Communication Skills
- Strategic Thinking Skills
- Leadership and Guidance
- Conflict Management
- Team Building
- Operational Management Skills

In addition to the above, I have also worked as music talent booking agent with William Morris Endeavor and as a stage manager with Production Resource Group, providing stage management for artists such as Alicia Keys and the Red Hot Chili Peppers. I received awards such as World Top 10 A&R representative of 2010, and booking agent of the year.

Throughout my thirteen years within this field, I feel I have the knowledge and experience necessary to enable you to accomplish your goal of giving me the "helping hand" I need to procure the best position in my career field. I would

155

appreciate meeting with you to discuss our mutual objectives. I look forward to your response.

Thank you in advance,

Name & Signature

SAMPLE COVER LETTER CRIMINOLOGIST

Name, address & email

Attention Search Committee:

I respectfully submit this cover letter and resume for the position of Criminologist for Vanguard Protective Services.

When _____ began in the year 2009, your main purpose was to provide personal protection for citizens using highly trained combat professionals as well as to cater to essential facets that one would expect from Law Enforcement Municipalities and The United States Secret Service. Just as any Law Enforcement agency, I am sure you seek intelligent, over-achieving, self-motivated, well trained professionals to be part of your team.

I currently hold a Master's Degree in Criminal Justice with a double Major in Psychology and a Minor in Oral Communications from the University of Miami and currently enrolled at Florida International University to obtain a PhD in the Criminal Justice field. For the past 14 years, I have worked in the Criminal Justice field and have held many Law Enforcement Supervisory positions such as a Correctional Officer Sergeant, Law Enforcement Captain and I currently hold the position as a General Inspector for Region IV offices. I work closely with the Secretary of State as well as the Chief Officer of all prisons to ensure that all facility operations are running smoothly and if there are any internal affairs that need to be addressed and resolved, I make sure immediate action is taken. Over the years I have acquired many skills that I strongly feel will contribute a great asset to your company. As a Criminal Justice major, I have developed the analytic al proficiency that is necessary for working through complex situations.

Included in your company vision statement, it states that you wish to reduce crime and make the world a safer place whether it is for celebrities or the everyday single mom who must hold two jobs to sustain a household. I feel confident that if given the opportunity, I can become a great asset to Vanguard Protective Services and make an immediate contribution to this establishment. I thank you today for allowing me to come before you and begin the interview process.

Sincerely,

_____

Jane Doe

Region IV General Inspector UM Alumni '09

SAMPLE COVER LETTER

COMPUTER ENGINEER

Name, Address & email Name, address & email

Attention Search Committee:

I respectfully submit this cover letter and resume for the position of computer engineer.

When _____ was founded in 1946, your main purpose was to become a popular aviation company that can last generations as well as be a company that represents a leap in technology, using the latest generation materials and design processes to reduce weight, improve performance and lower maintenance. As any corporation, I am sure you seek assiduous, ingenious, specialists to be a part of your company.

I currently hold a Masters Degree in Computer Science from the University of Central Florida. I have more than nine years of experience in the field of Computer Engineering. Some of my qualifications are:

- Computer Hardware Engineering certification
- Microsoft Certified Technology Specialist certification
- Analytical and problem solving skills
- Strong attention to detail
- Time management proficiency
- Effective communication skills

Throughout the last nine years of experience, I have gained the knowledge and experience needed to be a great asset to your corporation. I feel confident that given the opportunity, I can make an immediate contribution to your establishment. I would appreciate meeting you to discuss your goals and mutual objectives. I look forward to the employment interview.

Thank you in advance,

Name/Title/Signature

SAMPLE COVER LETTER

BUSINESS ADMINISTRATOR

Name, address & email

Attention Search Committee:

I respectfully submit this cover letter and resume for the Business Administer position.

When Createability Now Agency started in 2004 your purpose was to aid first-time business owners in their plans to succeed. As any organization, I am sure you seek hard working, intelligent, professionals to be a part of your team.

I currently hold a Master of Science degree in Business Administration from Cornell University. For the past five years, I have worked at Florida Power & Light overseeing their customer service department. Some of my qualifications include:

- Implementing business procedures
- Assessing employee performance
- Relating to customers
- Negotiating contracts and deals
- Mediating staff issues
- Interviewing and hiring staff

In addition to the above, I have comprehensive knowledge of payables, receivables, office administration and human resources. I am proficient in computer productivity software, departmental budgeting procedures and general management skills. Lastly, I possess excellent team work and communication skills. I have received several awards Outstanding Program of the Year in 2012 and the 2013 Diversity in Business.com nomination.

Throughout the last eight years, I have gained valuable knowledge and experience needed to be a great asset to your organization. I feel that given the opportunity, I can make an immediate contribution to your establishment. I would appreciate meeting with you to discuss your goals and mutual objectives. I look forward to the employment interview.

Thank you in advance, (Name/Title/Signature)

SAMPLE COVER LETTER CHEMIST

Name, address & email

Attention Search Committee:

I respectfully submit this cover letter and resume for the position of Chemist at your company.

When _____ started in 1985, your main purpose was to provide optimal cancer treatment for anyone and everyone through up-to-date research of technological advancements. As any organization, I am sure you seek hard working, intelligent, professionals to be part of your team.

I currently hold a Bachelor of Arts in Biochemistry from Vanderbilt University. For the past four years, I have worked in Memorial Sloan-Kettering Cancer Center in New York as a Cancer research specialty chemist. Some of my qualifications include:

- National Certification Commission in Chemistry
- Exceptional Problem solving skills
- American Cancer research license
- Global scientist research license
- Training in operation of high microscope equipment

In addition to the above, I have worked as a Cancer drug specialist for ten years with Mayo clinic and participated in the exploration of stem cell growth in aid to cancer at the John Hopkins hospital in Baltimore, MD. I have received countless awards for the advance studies of cancer treatment development operated by the American Cancer Society over the previous fifteen years.

Throughout the last twenty-five years, I have gained the knowledge and experience needed to be a great asset to your organization. I feel confident that given the opportunity to contribute to your company, I will greatly add to the prestige reputation affiliated with the International Cancer Medical Center. I would appreciate meeting with you to discuss your goals and mutual objectives. I look forward to the employment interview.

Thank you in Advance, (Name/Title/Signature)

SAMPLE COVER LETTER

FINANCIAL BANKER

Name, address & email

Date

Dear LBC Financial Corporation:

I respectfully submit this cover letter and resume for the position of a Financial Personal Banker. I have taken the liberty of enclosing my resume for your review. Thank you in advance for your consideration.

"Leading the employees on the path of achieving the company's objectives" is a mission that LBC Financial primarily considers. As any professional organization, I believe you seek for professionals with qualities such as hardworking, leadership, and problem solving.

I currently hold a Bachelor's Degree in Finance and Accounting from Florida International University. For the past four years I have worked at JPMorgan Chase & Co. as a Financial Manager. Some of my qualifications include:

- Prepare financial statements, business activity reports, and forecasts
- Supervise employees who do financial reporting and budgeting
- Monitor financial details to ensure that legal requirements are met
- Help management make financial decisions

In addition to the above, I was a member of Future Business Leaders of America in high school which is a nonprofit education association that prepares students for careers in business-related fields. Throughout the years I have earned various awards such as The Business Achievement award which focuses on basic business skills and community service dedication.

I can assure you that my knowledge, experience and leadership skills throughout the years will be a great asset to your company. I feel confident that if given the opportunity, my skills will contribute a great aspect to your company. I would appreciate meeting with you so that we may discuss your goals and objectives further. I look forward to the employment interview.

Thank you in advance,

Name/Title/Signature

SAMPLE COVER LETTER

COMPUTER INFORMATION SYSTEMS

Name, address & email

Attention Human Resource Manager

I respectfully submit this cover letter and resume for the position of Computer and Information Systems Manager.

The technical industry is rapidly changing and being on the cutting edge is a must. As I researched your organization I learned that one goal of Building Tech Industries is to create the most elaborate pressurizing equipment ever put into a commercial airplane and designed windows to resist being fatally blown out by cabin pressurization at 40,000 feet. This captivated my attention and what was even the more impressive is that your main purpose was to help college students find internships despite the failing job markets and difficulties due to the 2004 recession.

I currently hold a Master's degree in Computer Engineering from Northwestern University as well as in Business Administration from Syracuse University. For the past three years I have worked at Florida International University as an Assistant Professor teaching Computer science courses. Some of my qualifications include:

- Certified IT Consultant
- Contract Negotiation
- Problem Solving & Critical Thinking Skills
- Ergonomic Sensitivity
- C++ & Java Programming
- Planning and Organizing
- Exceptional Communication Skills

In addition to the above, I have also worked as a Project Manager for two years at Infinite Technology Solutions and as a Senior Software developer at Accenture CIO for three years prior. Some of my job duties included overseeing installation; ensuring back-up systems operate effectively; purchasing hardware and software; providing the ICT technology infrastructures for an organization. I have received numerous awards throughout my career such as becoming the Winner of the Howard J. Leonhardt New Venture Challenge and Technical Professional of the Year.

Throughout my eleven years within this field, I have gained the knowledge and experience necessary to be a great asset to your firm. I believe that given the opportunity, I can make a tremendous impact on the success of your organization. I would appreciate meeting with you to discuss your goals and mutual objectives.

Thank you for this opportunity, (Name/Title/Signature)

RESUMES

What is the purpose of a resume?

The purpose of a resume is to provide a summary of your skills, abilities and accomplishments. It is a quick advertisement of who you are. It is a "snapshot" of you with the intent of capturing and emphasizing interests and secures you an interview. It is not an autobiography. Since your resume is a primary tool in your job search, it needs to be carefully written and critiqued.

Writing Tips:

When preparing your resume, make sure it is **SHARP**.

The writing in your resume **should be concise, succinct**, and **to the point**. Use proper grammar, spelling, and punctuation in your writing.

Honest: You resume needs to be **factually accurate**, including dates of employment, education completed, job titles, and skills possessed.

Attractive: Your resume should be **visually appealing to the eye**. Make sure it is neat, organized, and consistent. Ensure you use enough "white space" by setting your margins at .5" or greater and providing ample space between sections.

Right: A resume should **reflect who you are and your professional experience**. This does not mean it should be laden with **unnecessary graphics or inappropriate personal information**; it means you should feel comfortable using it to represent yourself as a candidate.

Pertinent: Your resume and the way it is **organized should be relevant to the position**. Make adjustments to your resume based on the position you are applying.

WHAT'S THE DIFFERENCE? - KNOW THE DIFFERENCE!

Every college student should have the following:

1. A **resume.** It's a summary of what you have to offer an employer – it is a marketing tool. The product you are marketing is your value proposition – **what do you have to offer that distinguishes you from others with similar credentials**

2. A **professional biography** is a marketing tool used by **consultants, executives, and entrepreneurs** who are seeking work – it is commonly used for **"business-to-business" communication**. Like the networking profile, it is usually written as if someone were introducing you to a group.

3. A **networking profile** is generally a **single page summary that may be written in the "third-person," e.g., as if someone were introducing you to a group.** The profile is a useful networking tool – your contacts can easily review it and talk about you with others.

SAMPLE RESUME

IT FIELD

Name, address & email

COMPUTER INFORMATION SYSTEMS MANAGER

Software Development & Design | Management | Network Technology Consultant

Supervise other IT specialist. Prepare and direct technology-related activities, including software installation, computer programming, and network development and security. Responsible for updating, securing, and maintaining computer networks and assessing companies' operational needs. Oversaw hiring process and department inventory. Assign responsibilities to employees and supervise/participate in seminars. Certified Computer Repairer.

CORE LEADERSHIP QUALIFICATIONS

- Problem Solving Skills
- Critical Thinking Skills
- Java Programming
- Communication Skills

- Certified IT Consultant
- Certified Professional
- Ergonomic sensitivity
- Contract negotiation

- Planning and Organizing
- Reviewing and Evaluating
- Experienced Project Manager
- Multilingual
- C++ Program

PROFESSIONAL EXPERIENCE

FLORIDA INTERNATIONAL UNIVERSITY – MIAMI, FL   (DATE)

Assistant Professor – Computer Science

- Develop and execute inventive instructional methods
- Assess, supervise and mentor the academic progress in students
- Guide, direct and mentor research scholars in their research projects
- Review, assess and evaluate the activities and progress of students

Selected Accomplishments:

Winner of the Howard J. Leonhardt New Venture Challenge
FIU Torch Award- Outstanding Faculty, Excellence in Engagement Award

INFINITE TECHNOLOGY SOLUTIONS – SYRACUSE, NY   (DATE)

Project Manager

- Ensured that the Project Team completes the project
- Developed the Project Plan with the team and manages the team's performance of project tasks

Selected Accomplishments
Information Technology Executive of the Year
IT/Computer Systems Analyst Intern   (Date)

- Coordinated with teams to utilize technology to improve communication
- Contributed in improving functionality and profitability for computer systems

Selected Accomplishments
Awarded full time position as a Project Manager

ACCENTURE CIO -CHICAGO, IL   (DATE)
Senior Software Developer

- Wrote & Rewrote code
- Built automated tests

- Contributed to system architecture
- Mentored developers
- Contributed to development methodologies and standards for the team

Selected Accomplishments
Technical Professional of the Year
Green Enterprise IT Awards

UPS INFORMATION TECHNOLOGY DIVISION – GAINESVILLE, FL *(DATE)*
CO-OP Computer Programmer

- Converted applications to HTMLS
- Wrote codes

EDUCATION

Miami Dade College-Miami, FL
Associates of Arts Degree in Computer Science (Cum Laude),   *(DATE)*

University of Florida-Gainesville, FL
Bachelors of Arts Degree in Computer Science,   *(DATE)*
Bachelors of Science Degree in Information Management Systems,   *(DATE)*

Northwestern University-Evanston, IL
Masters of Arts Degree in Computer Engineering Science   *(DATE)*
Syracuse University-Syracuse, NY
Masters of Arts Degree in Business Administration   *(DATE)*

PROFESSIONAL CERTIFICATIONS AND AFFILIATIONS

Certifications: *(ONLY* if this applies to you)

Associate Computing Professional (ACP)
Certified Business Intelligence Professional (CBIP)
CITC - Certified IT Consultant
CCP - Certified Computing Professional
Microsoft.Net Certification Plus

Affiliations: (*ONLY* if this applies to you)

Association for Computing Machinery (ACM)

Institute of Electrical and Electronics Engineers (IEEE)

Electrical and Computer Engineering Department Heads Association (ECEDHA)

SAMPLE SCHOLARSHIP RESUME

The following scholarship information was retrieved from: www. georgetownisd.org/

Sample resume for college visits or college/scholarship applications; this is an example, include information that highlight YOUR STRENGTHS!

Name
Address
Phone # & Email

College Major/ Career Goal:	G.P.A. *(only if good)*
(include this only if you have one)	ACT: *same*
	SAT: *same*

Honors and Awards

- National Merit Semi-Finalist, (11)
- Lamp of Learning Academic Achievement Award (9, 10, 11)
- Missouri All State Choir, (10, 11)
- Miami All State Choir, (8, 9)

High School Activities

- Chiefs Yearbook Staff (10, 11, 12)
  - *Editor in Chief* (12)
- KHS Choir (9, 10, 11, 12)
- KHS Swim Team (10, 11, 12)
  - *Varsity Team Captain* (12)
- Spanish Club (9, 10, 11)

Community Activities

- Meals on Wheels Volunteer (Summers, 2003-Present)
  - Deliver 3-5 meals to senior citizens every Saturday throughout the year.
- Church Youth Group (9, 10, 11, 12)
  - Coordinated over 100 youth members for a 2-week mission trip.

Work Experience

- Kirkwood YMCA Summer Gymnastics Camp Instructor (*DATE*)
    - 20 hours per week during the school year and 45 hours per week in the summer.
- Kirkwood Library (2000-02)
    - Approximately 10 hours per week during the school year.

Interests

- Diving – Greenbriar Pool Dive Team (6 years)
- Dancing – Ballet, tap, jazz (10 years)

Please note: Follow the criteria the institution provides for the scholarship resume. This may vary pending on the establishment.

THANK YOU LETTER TIPS

THIS SHOULD DO THREE THINGS.

1. Thank them

2. Connect with them (*mission statement, vision or goals*)

3. Press for the position

SAMPLE THANK YOU LETTER

Name & Address

Dear Search Committee:

I would like to take the time and thank you today for giving me the opportunity to meet with you on April 19, 2012 regarding the position of Vanguard Protective Services Criminologist.

Allowing me to interview for this position increased my interest in working for your company. Allowing me to engage you in my future career goals as well as converse about our mutual objectives really made me feel that I can truly make a difference for your company. Your vision states (mention something about their vision and connect it to yourself). I am extremely confident that I can make an immediate and significant contribution to your company.

I am convinced that both my knowledge and experience will make me the best candidate for this position. I will bring excellent work ideas to the table at all times, and being there to motivate my fellow co-workers when at times we will feel under the pressure and of course I will make sure that my patients are taken care of at all times by providing them with the best treatment therapy I can offer. With the countless demands on your time, I am sure that you require people who can be trusted to carry out their responsibilities with minimal supervision.

Thank you once again for your time and consideration of my candidacy and allowing me to come before you on this day. I am looking forward to hearing from you soon and hopefully be working for your company in the near future.

Sincerely,

_____

Jane Doe

Chapter References

CHAPTER 1

Berman, J. (2009). Got work? College graduates face toughest job market in years. Hartford, Connecticut. Retrieved from http://abcnews.go.com/business/story?id=7636561

Burns, K. (2010). 50 biggest mistakes on a job interview. The amazing adventures of working girl: Real-life career advice you can actually use. Retrieved from US News and World Report: http://money.usnews.com/money/blogs/outside-voices-careers/2010/03/10/50-worst-of-the-worst-job-interview-mistakes

Dennis, K. (1998). What make the great, great? Strategies for extraordinary achievement. New York, NY. Crown/Archetype.

Feller, Rich, Ed.; Walz, Garry R., Ed. (1996). Career transitions in turbulent times: Exploring work, learning and careers. U.S. Department of Education and succeeding in the world of work. Retrieved from http://eric.ed.gov/?id=ED398519

Gala, L. (2011). Quote of the day. Retrieved from BrainyQuotes.com

Gottschalk, M. (2013, July 8). *Monet.usa.com.* Retrieved from Money Careers: http://money.usnews.com/money/blogs/outside-voices-careers/2013/07/08/6-ways-to unlock-your-creative-potential

Hughes, L. (2003, January 3). Retrieved from Poem hunter.com: http://www.poemhunter.com/poem/mother-to-son/

Kennedy, S. (2015). Stimulus jobs for new college grads. Retrieve from Monster College:http://career-advice.monster.com/job-search/company-industry-research/stimulus-jobs-entry-level-grads/article.aspx

Miami Dade College (2010). Center for community involvement service –learning overview. Retrieved from www.mdc.edu/cci

Mc-Graw-Hill, (2014). The big book of jobs. US Department of Labor: Bureau of Labor Statistics. McGraw-Hill Publications.

NACA (2015). Retrieved from NACE:https://www.naceweb.org/surveys/job-outlook.aspx

Owens, D. (2009). A purse of your own. Harford Connecticut: Howard Books Publications.

Pearson, J. (2003). Human communication. New York, NY: McGraw-Hill Publications.

Rachel Zupek, R. (2009). How social media can hurt your career. Retrieved from CareerBuilder.com:www.cnn.com/2009/living/worklife/08/24/cb.../index.html?

Robinson, M. (2015). *Top jobs for the future*. Retrieved from *www.careerplanner.com/Career-Articles/Top_Jobs.cfm*

Sai Knight Consulting (2012). The college savvy coach. Retrieved from Tag achives exxonmobile: http://www.siaknight.com/tag/exxonmobil/

Spencer, J. (1998). Who moved my cheese. In J. Spencer, *Who moved my cheese* (p. 93). New Jersey, U.S.A.: Putnam Pub Group.

Sharee, T. (2011). The importance of knowing how to sell yourself. Retrieved from Moguldom media group: http://madamenoire.com/84294/the-importance-of-knowing-how-to-sell-yourself/

Superville, D. (2010). Dateline Washington: Student loans get an Obama overhaul law makes government the primary lender. Associated Press. Retrieved from http://ccweek.com/article1723-dateline-washington:-student-loans-get-an-obama-overhaul;-law-makes-government-primary-lender.html

The National Association of Colleges and Employers (2009). Retrieved from NACE: http://www.naceweb.org/Research/Student/Student_Survey.aspx

Velmans, M. & Schneider, S. (Eds.). (2007). The Blackwell companion to consciousness. Northern Illinois: Wiley Blackwell, Publications.

Wolgemuth, L. (2009). 10 bets job for college students. Retrieved from http://www.usnews.com/topics/autho/liz_wolgemuth

CHAPTER 2- *BRIDGING THE GAP*

Adams, S. (2013). 5 mistakes college jobs seekers make. Forbes Staff. Retrieve from http://www.forbes.com/fdc/welcome_mjx.shtml

Balfanz, R., Bridgeland, J., Moore, L., &Hornig Fox, J. (2010). Building a grad nation: Progress and challenge in ending the high school dropout epidemic. Annual 2013 Update, Washington: Civic Enterprises. Retrieved from http://www.americapromise.org/sites/default/files/BuildingAGradNation2013Full.pdf

Bekerman, E. (2013). Quality manufacturing associates. Retrieved from http://webuildqualitytogether.com/author/admin/

Bersin, J. (2012). Growing gap between what business needs and what education provides. Leadership. Retrieved from http://www.forbes.com/site/joshbersin/2015/03/13/culture-why-its-the-hottest-topic-in-business-today/

Biecher, E., Keaton, P.N., & Pollman, A. W. (2015). Casual dress at work. S.A.M. Advanced Management Journal, 64(1), 17-20.

Bridgeland, J., Milano, J., & Rosenblum, E. (2011). Across the great divide: Perspectives of ceos and college presidents on America's. Retrieved from http://employmentpathwaysproject.org/wp-content/uploads/2014/04/Across-the-Great-Divide-Final-Report.pdf

Bridgeland, J., Milano, J., &Rosenblum, E. (2011). Across the great divide: Perspectives of CEOs and College Presidents on America's higher education and skills gap. Retrieved from http://www.corporatevoices.org/system/files/Across+the

Bureau of Labor Statistics, (2011). US department of labor, occupational outlook handbook. 2010-2011 Edition, OOH FAQs. Retrieved from http://www.bls.gov/oes/oes_ques.htm

Bureau of Labor Statistics, (2012). US department of labor, occupational outlook handbook. 2011-2012 Edition, OOH FAQs. Retrieved from http://www.bls.gov/oes/oes_ques.htm

Bureau of Labor Statistics, (2013). US department of labor, occupational outlook handbook. 2012-2013 Edition, OOH FAQs. Retrieved from http://www.bls.gov/oes/oes_ques.htm

Career Cast. (2010). *Jobs Rated.com: A Ranking of 200 Jobs from Best to Worst.* Retrieved from http://www.careercast.com/jobs/content/top-200-jobs-2010-jobs-rated. Clark, W.C., Kristjanson, P., Campbell, B., Juma, C., Holbrook, N.M., Nelson, G. & Dickson, N.M. 2010. "Enhancing food security in an era of global climate change: An executive session on grand challenges of the sustainability transition, San Servolo Island, Venice – June 6-9, 2010." *Center for International Development Working Paper,* Report198., (Sustainability Science Programe, Harvard Kennedy School, Cambridge, MA).

Coeling, H.V., & Wilcox, J.R. (2014). Steps to collaboration. *Nursing Administration Quarterly, 18*(4), 44-55.

College Parents of American (2013). Is your college students preparing for the world of work? Retrieve from http://www.collegeparents.org/members/resorurces/articles/

Dewey, C. (2012). Worst college majors for your career. Retrieved from http://www.kiplinger.com/slideshow/college/T0120S001-worst-college-majors

Dictionary.com (2013) Discovery News (2013). Discovery communications, Miami Dade College and Miami-Dade county public schools provide career exploration and job skills development opportunities for students.

Discovery Communications. Retrieved from http://corporate.discovery.com/ discovery-news/discovery-communications-miami-dade-college-and-mi/

Enger, R. & Jones, S. et al. (2008). Commitment to liberal education at the United States air force academy. Associations of American Colleges and Universities. Liberal Education Spring, 2010, Vol. 96, No.2.

Executive Office of the President, (2013). The president's climate action. The White House Office of Science & Technology. Retrieved from https://www.whitehouse. whitehouse.gv/sites/default/files/image/ president27sclimateactionplan.pdf

Farkas, K. (2012). College students' success increases when they are motivated by money officials say. The Plain Dealer. Retrieved from https://www.cleveland. com metro/ index.ssf/2012/12/college_students_success_incre.html

Flynn, C. (2011). How border security has change since 911. Michigan: Advisor & Source Newspapers. Retrieved from http://www.sourcenewspaper.com/ articls/2011/09/08 news/doc4e692ba174b59707800237.txt

Gearon, C. (2012). Healthcare industry offers jobs at entry level. US News Education. Retrieved from http://www.usnews.com/topics/author/ christopher-j-gearon

Gearon, C. (2012). Discover 9 new college majors with a future: Colleges are responding to workplace demand by adding degrees. US News Education. Retrieved from http://www.usnews.com/topics/author/christopher-j-gearon

Georgetown University Center on Education and Workforce, (2012). College is still the best Option. Retrieved from http://www9/geogetown.edu/grad/gppi/ hpi/cew/pdfs/collegepercent20stillpercent20bestpercent20option.pdf

Gordon, J. (2012). What college students need for long-term success? Founding Partner New Higher Education. Retrieved from http://www.openforum.com/ articles/4-capitals-college-students-need-to-start-growing-now/

Gordon, E. (2009). The global talent crisis. The Futurist: Retrieved from http:// www.imperialcorp.com/img/Futurist_article_9-09.pdf

Green Jobs: Toward decent work in a sustainable, low-carbon world. Retrieved from http://www.unep.org/PDF/UNEPGreenjobs_report08.pdf

Hart Research Associates. (2013). It takes more than a major: Employer priorities for college learning and student success-an online survey among employers conducted on behalf of: The association of American colleges and universities. Retrieved from https://www.aacu.org/sites/default/files/files/LEAP/2013_ EmployerSurvey.pdf

Hart Research Associates (2015). Optimistic about the future, but how well prepared? College students' views on college learning and career success. Hart Association Research, Washington. Retrieve from https://www.aacu. org/sites/default/files/files/LEAP/2015StudentSurveyReport.pdf

Hastings, R. (2012). Communication skills key for young workers. Retrieved from: http://www.shrm.org/hrdisciplines/employeerelations/articles/pages/communi cationskillskey.aspx

Heller, BR, Oros, MT, Durney-Crowley, J. (Jan. 2000). The future of nursing education. Trends to watch. Nurse Health Care Prospect. Retrieved from http://www.ncbi.nlm.nih.gov/pubmed/11040668

Heussner, K. (2013). Corporate America's next creative consultants? College kids om mindsumo. Retrieved from https://gigaom.com/2013/01/24/corporate-americas-next creative-consultants-college-kids-on-mindsumo/

Hill, S. (2007, October 18th). "24 tips for students to succeed in college" & "35 tips for students to succeed in Corporate America. Women's Edge. Retrieved from http://www.wook.pt/ficha/35-tips-for-students-to-succeed-in-corporate-america/a/id/1149637

Hughes, R. & Jones, S. (2011). Developing and assessing college student teamwork skills. Retrieve from http://onlinelibrary.wiley.com/doi/10.1002/ir.380/abstract

Hughes, S. (2013). The effect if casual dress on performance in the workplace. Master College. Retrieved from http://www.kon.org/urc/maloney.html

Humphreys, D. (2013). Employers more interest in critical thinking and problem solving than college major. Association of American Colleges and Universities. Retrieved from https://www.aacu.org/press/press-releases/

Kates, Robert, Thomas M. Parris, and Anthony A. Leiserowitz. 2005. What is sustainable development? *Environment* 47 (3): 9-21. [1.1] http://www.environmentmagazine.org/Editorials/Kates-apr05-full.html

Kuh, G. D. (2008). High-impact educational practices: What they are, who has access to them, and why they matter. Washington, DC: Association of American Colleges and Universities.

Lester, M. (2010). Six business skills every new graduate needs to develop. Monster Contributing Writer. Retrieve from http://career-advice.monster.com/in-the-office/starting-a-new-job/business-skills-for-new-graduates/article.aspx

Locke, G. (2011). STEM jobs help America win the future-The White House Blog. Retrieve from https://www.whitehouse.gov/blog/2011/07/14/stem-jobs-help-america-win-future

Lotto, J., & Barrington, L. (2006). Are they really ready to work? Employers' perspectives on the basic knowledge and applied skills of new entrants to the 21st Century US workforce. ERIC. Retrieved from http://eric.ed.gov/?id=ED519465

Lowe, N. (2011). Your professional image. Retrieved from http://www.slideshare.net/chattynattii/how-to-create-the-image-of-success

Marcus, J. (2013). States offer students an incentive to graduate: money. Washington: Higher Education. Retrieved from http://hechiStates offer students an incentive to graduatengerreport.org/states-offer-students-an-incentive-to-graduate-money/

Martin, N. (1995). Communication skills in the workplace employers talk back. Wake Technical Community College. Retrieved from http://www.sandhills.edu/academic-departments/English/teaching/comskills.html

McKinsey Global Institute, (June 2011). An economy that works: Job creation and America's future. Retrieved from http://www.mckinsey. com/mgi/publications/us jobs/pdfs/MGI_us_jobs_full_report.pdf

McPherson, W. (2015). "Dressing down" in the business communication curriculum. Business Communication Quarterly, 60(1), 134-146.

Hart Research Associates (2015). Optimistic about the future, but how well prepared? College students' views on college learning and career success. Hart Association Research, Washington. Retrieve from https://www.aacu.org/sites/default/files/files/LEAP/2015StudentSurveyReport.pdf

Occupational Outlook Handbook, (2012-2013). Retrieved from http://www.bls.gov/ooh/

Rodriguez, L. (20111). Privacy, security, and electronic health records. Office of Civil Rights. Retrieved from http://www.hhs.gov/ocr/office/about/rgn-hqaddresses.html

Taylor, M. (2010). Paths to professions. The Wall Street Journal, 12 (6), 5-18.

Turl, A. (2012). College students are going homeless and hungry: Corporate America is trying to exploit them. Alternet. Retrieved from http://www.alternet.org/college-students-are-going-homeless-and-hungry-and-corporate-america-trying-exploit-them

Saving for College, (2013). Savings 101.Merrile Edge. Retrieved from http://www.savingforcollege.com/articles/2013-1-year-top-performing-direct-plans

Schewbel, D. (2013). My 10 best pieces of career advice for college graduates. Retrieved from http://danschawbel.com/blog/my-10-best-pieces-of-career-advice-for-college-graduates/#sthash.kXIJV9E7.dpuf

Schroeder, R. (2010). Holding the Line for the 21 Century. US Customs and Border Patrol. Retrieved from http://www.cbp.gov/site/default/filles/documents/

Schroen, A. (2013). Miami dade college program develops students into researchers. Diverse Issues in Higher Education. http://diverseeducation.com/article/55099/

Turner. J (2014). A follow-up call wins the interview. Retrieved from http://career-advice.monster.com/job- interview/following-up/a-follow-up-call-wins-the-interview/article.aspx

U.S. Bureau of Labor and Statistics, (2010). Retrieved from http://www.bls.gov/

White C. M. (2013). The real reason new college grads can't get hired. Tie.com http://business.time.com/2013/11/10/the-real-reaso-new-college-grads-cant-get-hired/#ixzz2lJ8G8zZT

Whitman, L. & Kalil, T. (2015). A call for nanotechnology-inspired grand challenges. The White House Office of Science & Technology. Retrieved from https://www.whitehouse.gov/blog/2015/06/17/call-nanotechnology-inspired-grand-challenges

CHAPTER 3- SAY IT LIKE THIS!

Allhealthcare, (2013). 15 toughest interview questions and answers! Retrieved from http://allhealthcare.monster.com/careers/articles/3483-15-toughest-interview- questions-and-answers?page=7

American Sign Language, (2015). Retrieved from http:// www.nidcd.nih.gov/health/hearing/pages/asl.aspx

Andrews, E. (2013). 11 innovations that changed history. Retrieved from http://www.history.com/news/history-lists/11-innovations-that-changed-historyAnnual

Bentein, J. (2015). Virtural presence: Live visual streaming technology remotely connects experts to the field. Retrieved from http://www.newtechmagazine.com/index.php/internet-of-things/12424-virtual-presence-live-visual-streaming-technology-remotely-connects-experts-to-the-field

Berke, J. (2016). An Interview with the famous (now former) About.com deafness guide-Retrieved from -http://www.start-american-sign-language.com/jamie-berke.html

Boston University Arts & Science Program, (2016). Retrieved from http://www.bu.edu/biology/people/profiles/nelsa-estrella/

Boston Consulting Group (2014). Fashion and luxury companies struggle to find top talent, say industry experts. Retrieved from http://www.bcg.com/news/press/28april2014-fashion-luxury-companies-struggle-find-top-talent.aspx

Building a collaborative cultures (regardless of your size). (2015, February 27). Retrieved from http://www.inc.com/comcast/building-a-collaborative-culture-regardless-of-your-size.html

Business of Fashion (2015, January 16). Retrieved from http://www.businessoffashion.com/ Chiacu, D. (2015). Iranian hackers infiltrated computers that control New York dam. Washington D.C.: Reuters

Clymer, B. (2008). Research, publications and guidelines related to the use of internet to provide remote captioning or interpreting services for deaf students. Retrieved from http://www.ntid.rit.edu/sites/default/files/cat/VRI_References.pdf

Cofc_webmaster, (2012). SIFE students help restore oyster beds. *The College Today*. Retrieved from http://today.cofc.edu/2012/04/13/ sife-students-help-restore-oyster-beds/

Davis, G (2003). Handbook of gifted education. Boston, MA: Allyn & Bacon

Droste, T. (2015). Six steps to handling money questions. Monster Contributing Writer. Retrieved from http://career-advice.monster.com/salary-benefits/ negotiation-tips/six-steps-to-handle-money-questions/article.aspx

DiGiovanni, J. (2015). Common accounting mistakes beginners make and how to avoid them. Retrieved from https://www.fortis.edu/blog/online-degrees/ common-accounting-mistakes-beginners-make-and-how-to-avoid-them/ id/3444#sthash.BYzybmkZ.dpuf

Downing, M, (2014). Policing terrorism in the United States: The Los Angeles police department's convergence strategy. Retrieved from http://www. policechiefmagazine.org/magazine/index. cfm?fuseaction=display_arch&article_id=1729&issue_id=22009

Doyle, A. (2015). You're fired! How to handle getting fired. Retrieved from http:// jobsearch.about.com/od/salary/a/fired.htm

Dugan, D. (2014). 12 dos and don'ts for negotiating salary in a tough economy. Don't leave money on the tale just because times are tough. Salary.com. Retrieved from http://www.salary.com

Duke University (2016). Climate and energy program. Retrieved from https:// nicholasinstitute.duke.edu/

Giang, V. & Mondalek, A. (2013). 30 smart answers to tough interview questions. Business Insider. Retrieved from http://business.financialpost.com/ business-insider/30-smart-answers-to-tough-interview-questions

Gray, M. (2015). Producing more food with fewer resources. Retrieved from -http://www.sensatrack.com/

Gowrikumar (2013). The best answers to tough interview questions. Retrieved from http://www.gowrikumar.com/interview/index.php

Haag, A. (2016). Rightscorp provides solution to combat new peer-to-peer streaming app for music company's service combats aurous' illegal song sharing. Retrieved from http://www.prnewswire.com/news-releases/ rightscorp-provides-solution-to-combat-new-peer-to-peer-streaming-app-for-music-300148694.html

Heward, W.L. (2009). Exceptional children: An introduction to special education (9th ed.). New Jersey: Pearson.

Houston, N., Reilly, K.R., Greenwald, G., Cunning, D., & Deeter, A. (2014). Evaluation of a nurse-care management system to improve outcomes in patients with Complicated diabetes. Retrieved from http://care.diabetesjournals.org/ content/26/4/1058.full

Institute of veterinary animal & biomedical sciences. (2009, September, 20th). Retrieved from http://www.massey.ac.nz/massey/fms/Student%20services/Health%20and%20Counselling/Documents/CROW/Vets%20and%20Stress%20booklet%202009.pdf

Jenks, J (2016). Tactful answers to illegal interview questions Tips on protecting your right to privacy without jeopardizing a job offer. Retrieved from http://www.sfsu.edu/~sicc/documents/handouts/interviewing/Illegal_Questions.pdf

Joyce, S. (2013, Feb. 18) Job interview question: Why should we hire you? Work Coach Café. Retrieved from http://www.workcoachcafe.com/2013/02/18/job-interview-question-why-should-we-hire-you/

Kovacs, E. (2015). 61 million retail records lost in 2014: IBM Retrieved from http://www.securityweek.com/61-million-retail-records-lost-2014-ibm

Kokemuller, N. (2014). The definition of adaptability in the workplace. Retrieved from http://woman.thenest.com/definition-adaptability-workplace-14904.html

Legal Action Center (2011). Criminal records and employment. Retrieved from http://hirenetwork.org/sites/default/files/CriminalRecordsAndEmployment.pdf

Lindsay, N. (2006). How to knock your next interview out of the park. The Muse. Retrieved from https://www.themuse.com/advice/how-to-knock-your-next-interview-out-of-the-park

Lindsay, N. (2006). Great answers to tough interview questions. Retrieved from https://www.heidelberg.edu/sites/default/files/images/jfuller/GreatAnwerstoToughInterview Questions.pdf

Martin, C. (2014). Did you lose your job? Retrieved from http://blog.insurancejobs.com/interview-questions/did-you-lose-your-job/

Neil C. Rowe, N. (2016). Cebrowski Institute U.S. naval postgraduate school. Retrieved from http://faculty.nps.edu/ncrowe/edg_attacks.htm

Polus, S. (2013). Maryland lab artificially grows oysters for bay. Capital News Service. Retrieved from http://cnsmaryland.org/2013/11/12/maryland-lab-artificially-grows-oysters-for-bay/

Project MEET, (2013). Retrieved from https://drupalize.me/blog/201510/meet-project-manager-jeanne-cost

Report, Republic of South Africa (2013). Department of basic education. Retrieved from http://www.education.gov.za/LinkClick.aspx?fileticket=kiF59Co3OWA%3D

Resnikoff, P. (2014). The music industry has 99 problems. And they are... Retrieved from http://www.digitalmusicnews.com/2014/09/02/music-industry-99-problems/

Reynolds, R. (2015). Three categories of the hospitality industry. The Houston Chronicle. Retrieved from http://smallbusiness.chron.com/three-categories-hospitality-industry-58524.html

Satariano, A. (2013). The IPhone's secret flights from China to your local apple store Retrieved from http://www.bloomberg.com/news/2013-09-11/the-iphone-s-secret-flights-from-china-to-your-local-apple-store.html

SMART (2016). The association of wiping materials, used clothing and fiber industries since 1932. Retrieved from http://www.smartasn.org/index.cfm

Smith, J. (2014, April 7). Here's when you actually should discuss salary in a job interview. Retrieved from http://www.businessinsider.com/its-okay-to-discuss-salary-in-job-interviews-2014-4#ixzz3IyVq6Z47

Stringfellow, A. (2015). How to increase profit margins: 30 experts reveal the #1 way small business owners can improve profits. (July, 7). Retrieved from http://blog.directcapital.com/business-insights/how-small-businesses-owners-can-increase-profit-margins/

The National Consortium of Interpreter Education Centers (2009). Deaf interpreters in court: An accommodation it is more than reasonable Retrieved from http://www.interpretereducation.org/wp-content/uploads/2011/06/Deaf-Interpreter-in-Court_NCIEC2009.pdf

University of environment college of the environment. Biofuels. University of Washington (2016, January). Retrieved from https://environment.uw.edu/research/major-initiatives/biofuels/

Watson, A. & Fulambarker (2013). The crisis intervention team model of police response to mental health crises: A primer for mental health practitioners. US National Library of Medicine. Retrieved from http://www.ncbi.nlm.nih.gov/pmc/articles/PMC3769782/

Why is sustainability important for business? Co2 News. Retrieved December 2013 at: http://www.cawrecycles.org/californias-recycling-industry/

World Health Organization, (2014). Visual impairment and blindness. Retrieved from http://www.who.int/mediacentre/factsheets/fs282/en/

World Wear Project (2016). Textile recycling: Donating shoes and clothing never made more cents. Retrieved from http://worldwearproject.com/about-us

CHAPTER 4-YOU'VE GOT MAIL!

Retrieved from Livecareer.org
Retrieved from ResumeHelp.com
Retrieved from CareerPefect.com
Retrieved from Monster.com
Retrieved from Perfect Career.com
Retrieved from Resumehunter.com
Retrieved from Career Advice.com
Retrieved from Career Builder.com